SKILLS FOR BUSINESS ENGLISH

Student Book 3

Anne Dwyer

DELTA
PUBLISHING

Map of the book

UNIT	FUNCTIONS	SKILLS AND LANGUAGE FOCUS
1 The world of work *Employment*	Describing qualifications, skills and abilities Asking about and describing jobs and experience Describing employment conditions	A Reading • vocabulary: skills and abilities; an article giving advice on job interviews B Listening and reading • a recruitment process and selection criteria; matching job advertisements with commentaries C Writing and speaking • a letter of application; preparing for a job interview Role play: a job interview
2 From small beginnings *Company start-ups and growth*	Asking about and describing companies Requesting and checking information Describing growth Business plans	A Reading • vocabulary: running a business; an article about starting up a company B Listening • company histories; graphic descriptions of company growth C Speaking and writing • asking about companies; writing a press release Pair work: exchanging information about a company
3 Travel and trade *International commerce*	Comparing and contrasting Trade fairs Product presentations Comparing register and effectiveness	A Reading and writing • vocabulary: trade fairs; a report on trade fair participation; writing a report B Reading and listening • identifying fairs and services; preparing for business trips abroad and trade fairs C Speaking • product presentations; requests and offers Role play: at a trade fair
4 It's a cyber world *Information technology*	Describing the uses of computers and the internet Teleworking Writing e-mails Preparing short speeches	A Listening and writing • identifying different uses of information technology; writing an e-mail B Reading • teleworking – focus on cohesive devices; e-commerce and the internet C Speaking • speaking in public; opening lines; short speeches
5 Investment and growth *Finance*	Bank loans Raising capital Presenting and comparing investment opportunities Persuading people	A Listening • loan applications; investment profiles and approaches B Reading • financing a business; growing a business C Speaking and writing • presenting investment opportunities; persuading, promoting and comparing; writing a letter to a venture capitalist
6 Is it safe? *Health, safety and the environment*	Production and the environment Accidents Occupational health Describing processes	A Listening • globalisation and the environment; industrial accidents; discussing dilemmas B Reading • identifying role and functions of organisations; ergonomics C Speaking and writing • reporting back on a safety inspection; presenting and comparing case studies; writing a progress report

UNIT	FUNCTIONS	SKILLS AND LANGUAGE FOCUS
7 It's a deal *Negotiation*	Suggesting and requesting Arguing and hypothesising Negotiating	A Reading • cross-cultural negotiating styles; instructions for negotiating B Listening and writing • an interview about negotiating; courses related to negotiating; writing a request for information on a course C Speaking • identifying purpose within a negotiation; a questionnaire on negotiating Role play: a negotiation
8 Where's the market? *Marketing and sales*	Market research Discussing strategies Talking about sales trends Making proposals	A Listening • advantages of carrying out market research; developing a niche market B Speaking • vocabulary: graphs; describing trends; suggesting and comparing options Pair/group work: preparing and presenting oral reports C Reading and writing • television, the internet and advertising; the internet and niche markets; writing a proposal
9 Right place, right time *Logistics*	Making enquiries and complaints Checking progress and delivery Suggesting and discussing solutions	A Reading • logistics, distribution and supply chain management B Listening and writing • a sequence of phone calls relating to the fulfilment of an order; writing and replying to a letter of complaint C Speaking • the language of complaints in relation to delayed delivery Role play: negotiating a solution to a supply problem
10 Staying ahead *Knowledge management and competitive intelligence*	Discussing competitiveness Making and clarifying points Analysing opinions and situations	A Reading • vocabulary: staying ahead; knowledge management case studies B Listening • a knowledge management seminar C Speaking and writing • making and clarifying points; analysing opinions; writing an executive summary Role play: putting a company back on track
11 It's a free world *International trade*	Discussing international trade Reporting comments Describing conditions for foreign investment	A Listening • vocabulary: international trade; radio report of a WTO speech; global production and world trade in the future B Reading • free trade and protectionism C Speaking and writing • vocabulary: attracting foreign investment; relocating a manufacturing plant: comparing local conditions; writing a short report Role play: comparing two countries with a view to setting up a new factory
12 The bottom line *Budgeting and taxation*	Comparing and contrasting Exchanging information about figures Discussing problems and solutions	A Reading • vocabulary: accounting and taxation; an advertisement for tax services; budgeting advice; experiences with budgeting and taxation B Listening • vocabulary: budgeting and taxation; tax inspection; budgeting procedures C Speaking and writing • exchanging numerical information; accounting for and explaining figures; writing a performance report Role play: controlling a budget

The world of work

describing qualifications, skills and abilities

asking about and describing jobs and experience

describing employment conditions

KEY VOCABULARY

The skills and abilities listed below all appear in job descriptions in this unit. Work with your partner and talk about which of these apply to you. Then think of a job or two that would require each ability.

	You	Your partner	Job(s)
a head for figures	___	___	_____
the ability to work on your own	___	___	_____
analytical skills	___	___	_____
good communication skills	___	___	_____
computer-literate	___	___	_____
creative	___	___	_____
excellent time manager	___	___	_____
flair for working in a team	___	___	_____
organisational skills	___	___	_____
paperwork-oriented	___	___	_____

A Reading

1 Before you read, discuss the following:

- What should you do before a job interview?
- What should you do during an interview?
- What should you *not* do during an interview?
- What "tricky" questions might you be asked?

2 Now read the magazine article on page 5. It gives advice on how to prepare for a job interview. Choose the correct alternative to complete the sentences.

1 In job interviews, candidates tend to ignore the fact that _____.
   a) they are at a disadvantage
   b) they are buying and selling at the same time
   c) an interview is like a presentation
   d) the interviewer will be realistic

2 To prepare yourself for the interview, the writer _____.
   a) tells you to visit the competitors
   b) advises you to do research on the company
   c) says that you ought to prepare questions beforehand
   d) advises you to know little about the sector

3 When you go to the interview, make sure that you _____.
   a) are over-confident
   b) can make up your mind in four minutes
   c) are dressed in suitable attire
   d) do not arrive too early

4 The author states that _____.
  a) looking good does not give you an advantage
  b) nervous tics can put people off
  c) interviewers mistake aggressiveness for assertiveness
  d) smiling and eye contact are important

5 During the interview _____.
  a) you may need to think carefully about how to answer questions
  b) most tricky questions concern the personal life of the candidate
  c) the interviewer must put him or herself in the best light
  d) you should not talk about your rights

6 Which of the following is *not* expressed in the text?
  a) Short answers limit your chances of creating a positive impression.
  b) All over the world, candidates are expected to wear a suit to a job interview.
  c) Showing interest in a company may increase your chances of being offered a job.
  d) Interviewers can "read between the lines" (that is, they can understand more about us than we say).

Making the right impression

THE FIRST THING to remember when you go for a job interview is that this is not a one-sided affair. Treat it as you would a negotiation. After all, both you and the prospective employer are selling something. If you approach an interview with the attitude "any job will do", the interviewer will realise that immediately. If the job is worth anything, you won't get it.

You should prepare yourself for an interview just as you would do for a negotiation. Find out as much as you can about the company and the person who is to interview you. Don't be caught unawares. Go to the internet and look at the company's website. Compare it with that of its competitors. Alternatively, look at the Yellow Pages or trade magazines to see how they advertise themselves. Make enquiries at the Chamber of Commerce and other relevant organisations. Find out at least a little about the sector so that you can ask interesting questions.

Think of and note down your strengths and the opportunities that lie ahead. No matter how high unemployment is, regardless of how miserable you are in your current job, it's always an advantage to see things in a positive light. If you have little or no experience in a particular area, consider your capabilities in a similar area. Spend some time trying to imagine what type of employee the company is looking for and what makes you suitable for the job being advertised.

First impressions count, so look good and feel good before you go. Choose clothes that make you feel confident. Find out what clothes may put the interviewer off. Ensure you arrive at the interview with time to spare. According to more than one recruitment agency we spoke to, interviewees must understand the importance not only of their personal appearance but also of their body language. During the interview, breathe calmly and try not to appear too nervous. Look the interviewer in the eye and adopt similar body language to theirs. Smile and feel relaxed, enthusiastic and assertive. Remember one thing, though: assertive does not mean aggressive.

Don't just answer "yes" or "no" to questions. Treat every question as an opportunity to demonstrate that you are suitable for the job, but remember to stick to the point. When asked about your interests, include group as well as individual activities/hobbies. Be on the lookout for tricky questions about your personal life. You don't need to lie; just sell yourself in the best light. This is something the interviewer needs to be able to do as well. You have the right to find out whether or not you want to work for the company. Furthermore, your interest in the nature of the company and how it is run may well end up being your big selling point.

Listening and reading

1 🎧 Listen to a recruitment officer for the National Westminster Bank (a large British bank) describing the company's recruitment procedure in his country. Mark the statements T (for true) or F (for false).

1	Recruitment officers try to spot potential top managers while they are still at university.	T	F
2	Not all graduates want to become managers.	T	F
3	What people study will help them to get a job in a bank.	T	F
4	Social activities may count as much as academic achievement.	T	F
5	Good all-round performers have a better chance of getting an interview.	T	F
6	Candidates with an exceptional academic record are never selected for an interview.	T	F

2 Listen again and complete the summary below using a number or up to three words for each gap.

WHEN AND WHERE?

At the National Westminster Bank (NatWest), recruitment takes place from
January to March at universities around the country.

ANNUAL INTAKE

There are several levels of recruitment. First of all, they take on

approximately (1) _____ recruits who will probably become

(2) _____ or (3) _____ within about ten years.

Secondly, they select a much smaller group of about (4) _____

recruits known as (5) _____, who are earmarked to become

CEO (chief executive officer), deputy CEO or (6) _____ when

they reach the height of their career. They also take on two other groups,

50-odd (7) _____ who do not want to become managers and

some other graduates formerly recruited among the school-leaver market.

CHARACTERISTICS OF SUITABLE CANDIDATES

Pre-selection is done based on information submitted by interested

candidates on an application form. On the whole, the bank is interested

in all-rounders, rather than people who only have excellent

(8) _____. Their degree subject is (9) _____.

To be considered, interested candidates should be taking or have taken

part in union activities and/or (10) _____.

---

3 Discuss these questions in pairs or threes.

- Are recruitment procedures similar in your country/sector?
- How effective do you think this system is?
- What do you think about the criteria upon which candidates are pre-selected by NatWest?

4 Look at the sentences below and at the jobs being advertised. Which job(s) does each sentence refer to? For each sentence, mark one or more advertisements.

A

EXECUTIVE SECRETARY

We wish to appoint an executive secretary to manage the final year of a major academic project in a leading business school. The post is partly paperwork-oriented, and duties will include co-ordinating the director's workload, correspondence, dealing with day-to-day bureaucracy, managing the budget (invoices, expenses and so on), writing up reports, making meeting and travel arrangements, developing websites, keeping a record of borrowed books and articles, and so on.

You will be an efficient team member with initiative and good organisational skills. You will know how to be diplomatic and filter correspondence and contacts, especially when the director is absent. You will thus need to be proficient in word-processing, accounting and database software programs as well as in the use of the internet.

B

URGENT

MARKETING SERVICES ASSISTANTS REQUIRED

We are a dynamic, rapidly expanding company and are now looking for graduates for our Marketing Services Department. Our team is full of talented, creative, dynamic people who are encouraged to innovate and whose skills and contribution are valued.

The right applicants will be responsible for the collation and analysis of data we receive from our customers. You will need to have a head for figures and a good grasp of spreadsheets. In other words you will be computer-literate and highly numerate, with strong analytical and communication skills. You will be an excellent planner and time manager, able to work to tight deadlines. An ability to work on your own as well as in a team is essential.

C

IT Support Person

We wish to employ an IT person to support our partnership of international economics consultants. Responsibilities will include developing business notes in our office systems programme and managing our network. The position requires someone who has some experience with IT systems and can demonstrate an ability to make a rapid contribution to our business performance. Knowledge of at least one widely used language other than English is a must, as the successful applicant will go on short overseas assignments to establish and support IT systems for our international project offices. In return, we offer a competitive salary with profit-related bonuses, not to mention the opportunity to join a stimulating and successful company.

1 You need to be good at maths to get this job. ____

2 If you are not an experienced user of the world wide web, do not apply. ____

3 If the company does well, you'll earn more. ____

4 You need to be able to work on your own. ____

5 You have to be willing to travel. ____

6 If you don't know how to be tactful, do not apply. ____

7 You have to be a good at organising your time in this job. ____

5 🎧 Listen to three extracts in which people refer to the jobs advertised. Match the jobs with the conversations.

1 ____   2 ____   3 ____

6 Now listen again and match the extracts with the situations below. You will not need to use all the situations.

a) Someone enquires about a job. ____

b) Someone has been asked to submit proof of CV details. ____

c) Someone has been offered a job. ____

d) Someone wants to turn down a job. ____

e) Someone is being interviewed for a job. ____

Covering letter for a job application

The key objective of a covering letter is to inform the prospective employer of your interest in and suitability for the job. In the letter, you will need to make yourself look professional, build goodwill and offer a glimpse of your personality.

The greeting: If possible, find out the name of the person who is going to read the letter. Alternatively, use the *Dear Sir/Madam* or *To Whom It May Concern* formulae.

The opening of the letter should sound positive and enthusiastic. It must include a reference to the job being sought and should mention how you found out about the position (the more personal the better, especially if somebody you know has suggested that you apply for the position).

The body of the letter should contain from one to three paragraphs and must answer the question: Why should you be selected for the job? So in terms of content, you will need to describe your skills and personality traits and say why and how they can benefit the employer.

The close: Refer to your CV and any other attachments being included. Be action-driven and request an interview. State when and where you can be reached.

End appropriately, eg *Yours sincerely*.

1 Look at the covering letter below. Check to see that it follows the tips above.

---

24 Kimberley Road
Sheffield S2 2AD

Ms K Amiksson
Human Resources Department
ETM Ltd
Taylor House
Clifton Road
Nottingham NG25 0PR

Dear Ms Amiksson,

I am most interested in applying for the position of Junior Product Manager advertised in the Canterston University Job Centre. Gordon Jeffers' description of your company and the job made the position sound like an exciting opportunity, and one which seems to match my skills and experience.

I am about to complete my degree in Business Administration at the university and am eager to work for a company with a proven track record in its sector. Part-time employment has given me useful insights into the working world and I have been able to apply what I have learnt on the job to my studies and vice versa. This is one of the reasons I feel I would be suitable for the position you are offering.

I have also taken part in university activities. I am a member of the tennis club and play for one of the university's basketball teams as well. I play the guitar and am an active member of the BdaB Jazz Club.

I am imaginative and reliable. I have an analytical mind and up-to-date computer skills. I speak two foreign languages quite fluently (French and Arabic).

In support of my application I have attached my CV and references. I am keen to pursue this application and would appreciate the opportunity to discuss my application in an interview. I can be reached during business hours on 609 399 299.

Yours sincerely,

Hannah Price

Ms Hannah Price

2 Write a covering letter for one of the jobs on page 7.

3 In a job interview, the interviewer may ask a wide range of questions. Below are some questions that are often asked. In pairs, discuss how you would answer the questions in an interview.

- What would you say are your (most significant) educational achievements?
- What did you learn while you were studying that will help you in this job?
- Can you describe if and how you met deadlines while you were studying?
- Would you be willing to undertake training, even if this takes place in your free time?
- What are your greatest professional achievements to date?
- To what extent are you analytical and/or creative and could you give us an example to demonstrate this ability?
- Do you prefer to work on your own, or as part of a team?
- What qualities do you think this job requires?
- Why do you think we should employ you?
- Where do you want to be in ten years' time?

4 Are there any questions in Exercise 3 you did not wish to reply to? Give reasons. Think of other questions you could be asked and how you would reply.

5 This role play is for two speakers.

Choose one of the jobs mentioned in this unit or choose an advertisement from another source (eg a newspaper, the internet).

A is applying for the job. B works for a recruitment agency and will interview A.

A looks at this page. B turns to page 76.

SPEAKER A

The job you have applied for is one of three you have been shortlisted for. Decide why you would be suitable for this job and how you would answer questions like those in Exercise 3 above.

You are looking for a job with an above-average salary and good prospects for promotion, in a company which values its employees. You would like to start your new job after the summer break as you have planned (and paid for) a holiday in Australia in August.

Ask about:
- salaries
- working hours (some companies offer four-day working weeks in summer)
- fringe benefits
- promotion possibilities
- whether you will work in a team
- when the job starts

From small beginnings

asking about and describing companies

requesting and checking information

describing growth

business plans

KEY VOCABULARY

Complete the definitions below with words or expressions from the box. You may have to alter the terms to make the definitions grammatically correct.

> cash flow management   break even   facilities   capitalisation
> lending agency   executive summary   cash flow   premises

1   In its role as a _____ a bank lends money for a number of purposes and in different forms which include mortgages, start-up loans and overdrafts.

2   When calculating the viability of a business, the future businessperson needs to forecast how much money will be coming into the company and how much is going to be spent on purchases and overheads. This movement of money is called _____.

3   _____ involves planning and distributing this income and expenditure so that there is no shortage of money at any one stage.

4   When income is equal to expenditure (in other words, when a company is neither making a profit nor a loss), we say the company is

_____.

5   _____ normally refer to buildings where economic activity takes place.

A   Reading

1   Answer these questions before you read.

1   What do you think the average failure rate is among new businesses?
2   What is a business plan and what does it consist of?
3   How long should it be?
4   How long can it take to write?
5   Why is it necessary to have a plan?

2   Now read the text on page 11, which is about setting up a business. It comes from a booklet for aspiring business owners and entrepreneurs. Choose a suitable heading for each section from the options given.

3   Go back and look at the questions in Exercise 1 again. Have your answers changed?

4   Which of the following is the best summary of the text?

a) If would-be entrepreneurs do not have a business plan they are likely to fail.
b) A business plan can help to guide a would-be entrepreneur along a safer route to profitability.
c) A business plan guarantees success.

Ⓐ THE UNITED STATES: SUCCESS FACTORS / BUSINESS START-UPS: THE FACTS / SMALL BUSINESSES

According to a recent poll, one in every four Americans thinks about creating their own company and every year, one million people in the United States do start a business. Of those new business ventures, a third last less than six months, and by the end of the first year 40 per cent will have closed. Between 75 and 80 per cent of new small businesses close by the end of the fifth year and fewer than 10 per cent will last longer than ten years.

The average small business owner fails almost four times before finally succeeding. Nonetheless, there are statistics to support the American dream: according to the United States Internal Revenue Service, 89 per cent of citizens earning more than $50,000 per annum are small business owners.

Ⓑ THE CAUSES OF FAILURE / THE SYMPTOMS OF FAILURE / THE RATIONALE OF FAILURE

Businesses fail for a variety of reasons. The most commonly cited reasons are lack of experience coupled with lack of basic marketing and budgeting skills; under capitalisation; poor cash flow management; poor choice of location; incompatibility of personality with the business or with partners – in short, a lack of business knowledge.

Ⓒ LIVE AND LEARN / HOW TO START / BUSINESS PRACTICE

There are at least three ways to gain business expertise. One way is to buy into a franchise. A well-organised business franchise operation sells much more than a product: it sells a system to succeed in the business. Another method is trial and error. Failing in business becomes a lesson learned. However, the most effective way is to learn from others.

Ⓓ PAPERWORK FIRST / OBTAINING FINANCE / PLANNING IS ESSENTIAL

Many business failures could have been avoided if the potential entrepreneur had thought out and written up a business plan beforehand. Often referred to by consultants as "roadmaps to success", business plans can be vital, not only when starting up a business but throughout its life cycle. Most lending agencies require a detailed business plan before even considering a request for a start-up or growth loan. Comprehensive yet easy-to-follow business plans serve not only to procure loans; they also have an invaluable diagnostic and developmental role to play in the early stages and later growth of a company.

Ⓔ SUMMARIES / THE CONTENTS OF A BUSINESS PLAN / WHAT THE BUSINESS PLAN DOES

The plan should start with a short but engaging executive summary followed by a bird's eye view, rather than a technical description of the company. This will specify the sector, location and purpose of the company as well as briefly describing the state of the industry.

The remainder of the plan falls under three subheadings: **Operations**, **Marketing** and **Finance**.

Operations means detailing production requirements, facilities, flexibility and know-how.

Marketing will have two separate sections. First there will be an analysis of the demand and competition in the market. Secondly strategy will be described.

The **financial plan** includes an analysis of profitability, cash flow, break even, cash and capital management and financial arrangements and projections. There should be a narrative description supported by realistic financial calculations.

This will be followed by a summary, a conclusion and appendices with names of customers, references, qualifications and so on. All this should be presented in a logical order and be no longer than 25 pages. The plan should be written bearing in mind who and what the plan is for.

Ⓕ SOURCES OF ADVICE / PROCESS AND PRODUCT / TIMES HAVE CHANGED

The planning process is as important as the plan itself, if not more so. It is estimated that it takes an average of 200 hours to write a good business plan. Getting advice is essential. In the past, bank managers would sit down with a client and talk things through. Many banks do have a department to help people get started, some offer workshops, and many offer free start-up guides. But advice is often sought elsewhere. There are several good sites on the internet. Business associations and government bodies often have a free or low-cost advisory service. Accountants and business consultants can also be contracted to help assess and consolidate ideas.

Whatever option is chosen, the aspiring business owner must feel comfortable with the advice giver.

5 Discuss the text in pairs. Does anything surprise you? Would you add any other advice? Apart from planning, what elements do you consider to be the most important for business success?

B Listening

The vocabulary below will help you to understand the five case studies presented in this section. Match the words on the left with the definitions on the right.

1	sole trader	A	a business partnership formed for a particular purpose
2	hallmark	B	a company owned by one person
3	joint venture	C	rent a property or machine
4	mill	D	a template, cast form or shape which is used to make identical objects
5	mould	E	a factory or building with machinery for grinding wheat, processing wood pulp, etc
6	lease	F	a mark or characteristic of excellence
7	takeover	G	gross sales
8	turnover	H	when one company buys a controlling interest (over 50%) in another

1 🎧 Listen to five extracts which describe the development of five companies. Identify the sector each company operates in. Choose from options A–G.

1 ____	A automobile components
2 ____	B food
3 ____	C hotels and restaurants
4 ____	D household appliances
5 ____	E leasing and rentals
	F plastics
	G real estate

2 Listen to the extracts again. Match the statements below with the extracts. There are two statements for each extract.

a) If this company had not changed its strategy it might not have survived. ____

b) The company has had few, if any, industrial accidents. ____

c) The owner's expansion strategy was counterproductive. ____

d) The owners of this company sold it to a larger concern. ____

e) This company's success started with a trip abroad. ____

f) The owners were not able to handle a larger version of the business. ____

g) This business belongs to a sole trader. ____

h) This company was given a prize for the design of its products. ____

i) This family company is still making the product that changed the course of the business. ____

j) The owners sold out and are no longer involved in the business. ____

3 🎧 When talking about company growth, a number of areas can be focused on, eg turnover, production, productivity, number of outlets, branches, factories. Can you think of any others?

Listen to five short extracts in which the growth of companies is described. First match each extract with one of the graphs on page 13. (One of the graphs is not used.) Then write down the words and phrases you hear that justify your answers.

A ___

Market share – sunglasses

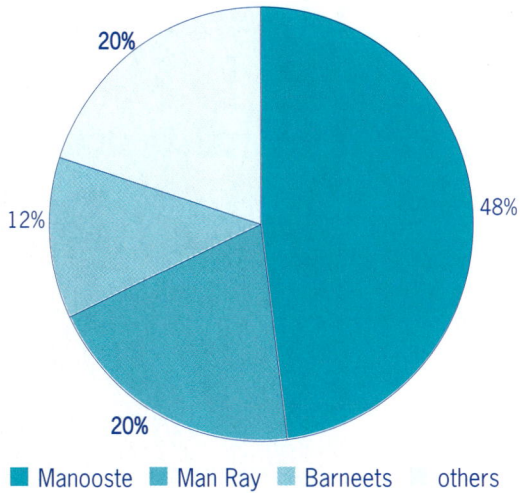

20%
48%
12%
20%

■ Manooste ■ Man Ray ■ Barneets others

B ___

Market share – sunglasses

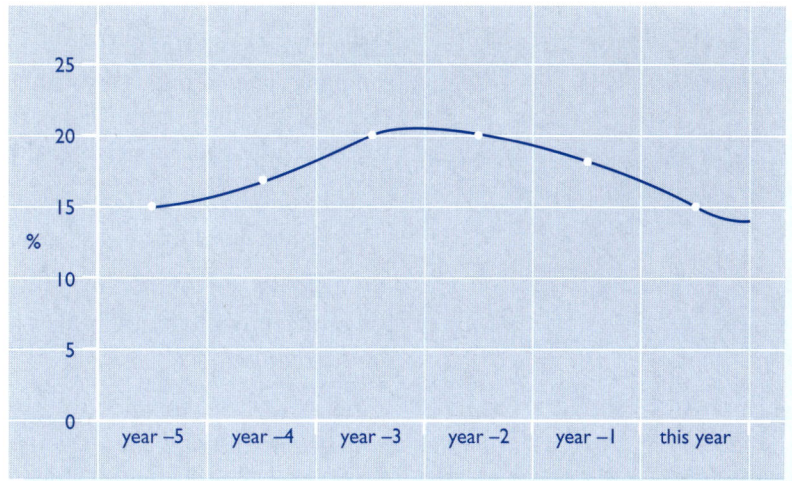

%

year –5   year –4   year –3   year –2   year –1   this year

C ___

Sales and overheads

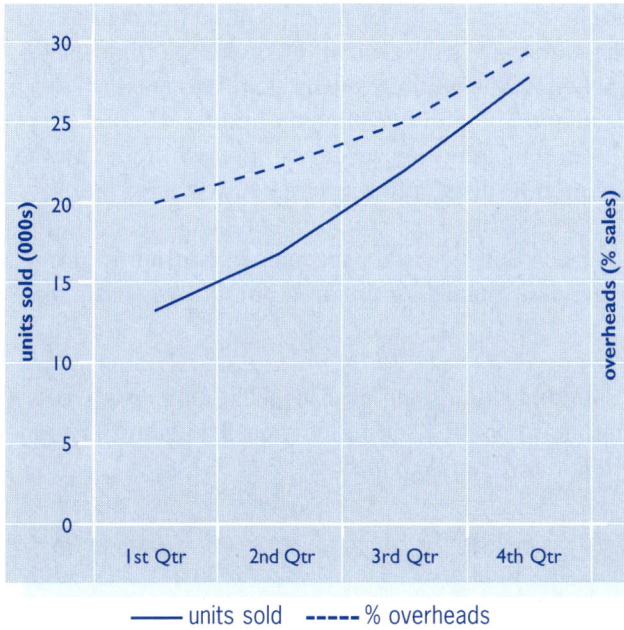

units sold (000s)

overheads (% sales)

1st Qtr   2nd Qtr   3rd Qtr   4th Qtr

——— units sold   ----- % overheads

D ___

Number of outlets

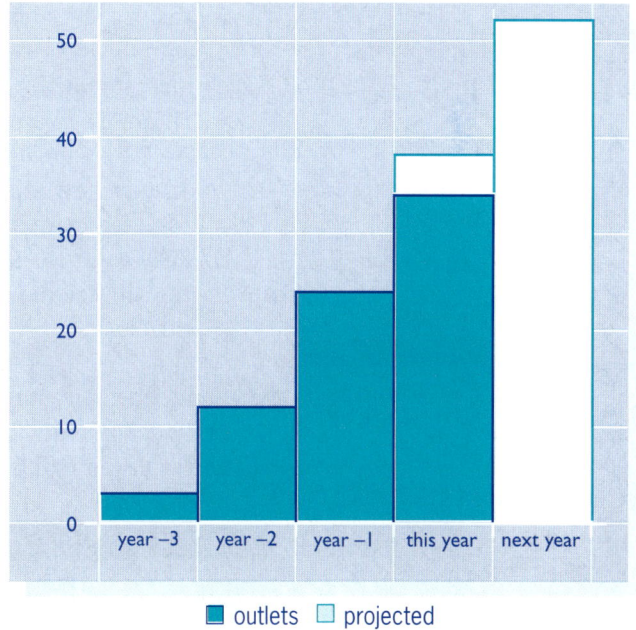

year –3   year –2   year –1   this year   next year

■ outlets □ projected

E ___

Cement sales: South American Division

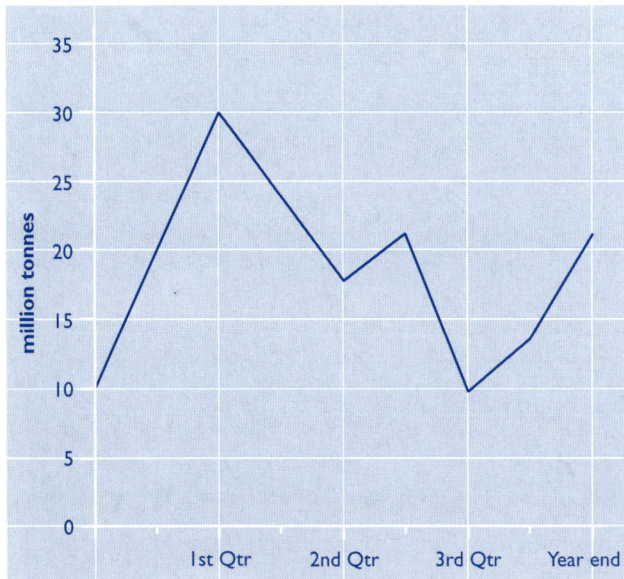

million tonnes

1st Qtr   2nd Qtr   3rd Qtr   Year end

F ___

Sales and labour productivity

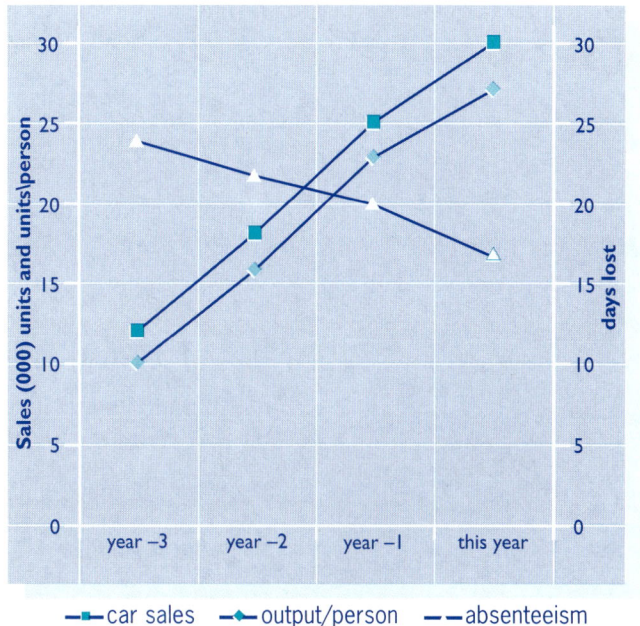

Sales (000) units and units\person

days lost

year –3   year –2   year –1   this year

—■— car sales   —◆— output/person   —— absenteeism

C Speaking and writing

1 Look at the information below about the past, present and future of a bicycle manufacturing company. The company was founded in 1976 and was initially a family concern. It went public 19 years later and has grown steadily since then.

In pairs or small groups, decide what questions would generate the answers given.

For example:
It manufactures folding bicycles. – *What does the company do?*

1 In 1976.
2 It started out as a family concern, but now it trades its shares on the stock exchange.
3 Since 1995.
4 Well, the company grew steadily for the first five years or so and then there was a downturn in business for a few years.
5 Yes, it did. Sales, for example, have gone up an average of 15 per cent per annum since it went public, and there's now a staff of about 1,500 plus sales representatives, whereas when it was a family business, it was smaller.
6 There are two plants in Thailand and another one in Vietnam.
7 Well, they have distributors in Asia and they've started going to trade fairs to capture new markets and find new distributors, so they now have a few affiliated companies around the world. They sell on-line as well.
8 They want to enter new markets outside Asia, especially in Northern Europe.
9 Yes, they're developing some new models for children and others for senior citizens.

2 Sometimes direct questions sound abrupt. Using phrases like *Can you tell me ...?* or *Do you know ...?* can sound more polite. Go through your list again starting each question with *Can you tell me ...?* or *Do you know ...?*

KEY EXPRESSIONS

Requesting information

Can you tell me something about how the company started up?
Can you give me any information regarding their annual turnover?
What do you know about their distribution?
Can you tell me how many outlets they opened in 1986?

Checking information

According to my figures, the annual turnover is $18 million. Can you verify that/Is that figure correct?
Let me check that again: did you say 18 million – one eight?
Sorry, I didn't quite catch that. How much did you say?

3 This pair work activity is for two students.

You and your partner will receive information about a textile company. The fact sheets are not complete.

Ask each other questions to get a more complete picture of the company.

A looks at page 15. B turns to page 76.

SPEAKER A

PRESS CONFERENCE FACT SHEET
Zara International

ORIGINS
Zara or **Zara International** is the flagship of **Inditex**, a group made up of 60 different companies, not all of which are in textiles. The company, whose major shareholder is _____, started up as a manufacturer of housecoats and pyjamas in _____ in Galicia, Spain. It operated initially out of a small _____. So successful was this first venture that Ortega left his job with a shirt company and expanded the business. During the economic slump in the early seventies he bought out ailing textile manufacturers and set up Inditex. The first Zara outlet opened in 1975.

FIGURES
Outlets: Every _____ a new Zara shop opens up somewhere in the world. (1998 figures)
The group had 24 outlets in _____, 622 in 1996, _____ in 1997 and 740 (483 in Spain, 257 elsewhere) in 1998. Average investment per outlet was 3 million euros.

The **annual turnover** in 1985 was 30 million euros; in 1997 it was 1.12 billion euros and in 1999 _____.
The group generates a daily **net profit** of more than 0.4 million euros. Between 1994 and 1999 sales doubled and net profit _____.
The group employed 11,000 people in 1996; 12,000 in 1997.

Distribution: Orders are met within two weeks. A fleet of more than 60 trucks plus several company aircraft distribute new merchandise twice weekly to the stores. Warehouses are emptied _____ more often than the sector average.

SALES
55% Spain, 33% Europe, 8% Latin America, 4% rest of the world

FUTURE PLANS
The company aims to create a retail network across Europe. They plan to open 160 new stores over the next three years and forecast a _____ increase in turnover.

---

4 Here is a press release about Nawoyo, the bicycle manufacturer. In what order are the following points mentioned?

a) description of the company _____

b) future plans _____

c) historical background _____

d) manufacturing and distribution _____

e) organisation and staff _____

f) sales and profit _____

The Nawoyo Trading Company is a leading manufacturer of folding bicycles. Established in 1976, the company started out as a family concern, but went public in 1995. Since then sales have increased by an average 15 per cent per annum and the staff has grown from 800 to 1,500 employees, excluding sales representatives. The company has three factories, two of which are located in Thailand. The third factory is in Vietnam. In a bid to expand internationally the company has taken an active part in international trade fairs and has set up an on-line purchasing facility. New product ranges of bicycles for children and for senior citizens are expected to be launched in the near future.

---

5 Taking the text in Exercise 4 as a guide, write a press release (100–120 words) about Zara International. Use the information about the company which you gathered in Exercise 3. Include at least two graphs.

Travel and trade

comparing and contrasting

trade fairs

product presentations

comparing register
and effectiveness

KEY VOCABULARY

Look at the words *in italics* in the report below. Match them with the following definitions or synonyms.

a) all-in package deals where everything is done for you
b) designed to attract
c) extras
d) paying someone (or a company) to do a task for you
e) the style of language used when promoting a product

A Reading and writing

1 Jason Needham has recently joined a small company with little experience in exporting. He is responsible for sales and marketing, in particular increasing the company's export sales. He has written the following report about trade fairs. Read the report and choose the correct alternative to fill each gap.

To: Paul Christiansson

From: Jason Needham

Subject:

Exhibiting at trade fairs

The purpose of this report is to examine alternatives for promoting our company and its goods at trade fairs abroad.

TYPES OF FAIRS
Exhibitions range from small one-company promotions to mega-events held in large open indoor spaces that (1) _____ hangars at an airport. There are specialist fairs aimed at companies in specific sectors and smaller regional events, which are often open to and *targeted at* the consumer. The latter tend to be multi-sector fairs.

OPTIONS
Goods and services can be exhibited in a number of ways. Companies with stands either use the services of specialists to (2) _____, or organise things themselves. There is a third option to consider: (3) _____ of what is known as an "umbrella stand" under the auspices of a government or trade organisation.

OUTSOURCING
Outsourcing means contracting specialised consultants who offer both *turnkey operations* and a choice of smaller packages. Most advisors recommend meeting before planning anything. In this way the style of the stand can be more easily fine-tuned to (4)

_____ the company's aims and objectives while taking into account local values. Planning early also leaves time to discuss "*add-ons*" which the company might find attractive. These (5) _____ creating special lighting effects, audio-visuals, promotional items like pens and ties, and even organising outside events. Advice will be given on cultural aspects, technical matters and so on. (6) _____ companies can also mail potential clients in advance. The advantage of using consultants lies in their expertise and their ability to arrange things like negotiating the best location for the stand. The (7) _____ is the cost. This is the most expensive option.

DOING IT OURSELVES
At some fair venues, "shell schemes" can be rented. They (8) _____ the walls, a sign and some furniture. As a rule, shell schemes have no "frills", but they are affordable. (9) _____ of the features described in such packages, all measurements, audio-visual and electrical specifications must be checked in advance, as not all countries use the same system. Experts say that it is essential to find out about the type of public that is likely to attend and about the local standard *sales pitch* and plan things according to local schedules. To maximise possibilities, the company should get in (10) _____ with potential clients before arriving. Advice on the above matters can often be sought (11) _____ from tourist boards, national airlines, the commercial service at the embassy, the chamber of commerce and so on. Most

experts consulted agree that a company (12) _____ organise a stand on its own but state that this is very time-consuming and can go wrong. Furthermore, they point out that pavilion space is not always allotted on a "first come first served" basis.

UMBRELLA STANDS
Umbrella stands are set up under the auspices of a government body or trade organisation. They are a way of taking part at very low cost. The disadvantage of umbrella stands is that displays frequently go unnoticed, as the stands are often crammed with bits and pieces belonging to a wide range of participants. (13) _____, they do give an insight for future reference and can be used as a springboard to network and do business.

OTHER INFORMATION
Most large trade fairs have websites where (14) _____ of stands are published. In fact these websites are somewhat like virtual exhibitions. The essential difference between visiting an exhibition on the internet and going to the fair itself is that the latter is where public relations take place and PR can be a vital selling point.

RECOMMENDATION
I recommend that we start off either as part of an umbrella stand or outsourcing the organisation of the stand. The cost of the former is significantly lower than the latter, but outsourcing will probably bring better results. In the future we may be able to take over the organisation ourselves.

1 a) look   b) similarise   c) resemble   d) are as
2 a) set everything   b) set everything up   c) set up all   d) set all
3 a) forming part   b) participating   c) taking part   d) belonging
4 a) include   b) match   c) pair with   d) absorb
5 a) consist in   b) contain   c) include   d) are
6 a) Like   b) Those   c) These   d) The such
7 a) drawback   b) contrary point   c) worst   d) trouble
8 a) have to include   b) used to have   c) usually include   d) may have
9 a) Despite   b) Regardless   c) No matter   d) In view
10 a) connection   b) combination   c) contacts   d) touch
11 a) costless   b) priceless   c) charge-free   d) free of charge
12 a) should   b) might   c) can   d) must
13 a) Although   b) Indeed   c) Nonetheless   d) Despite
14 a) information   b) commercials   c) the feature   d) details

WRITING TIPS

Long reports

Long reports are accompanied by an **executive summary**, in which the purpose, the main findings and recommendations are summarised.

The **introduction** must define the purpose and terms of reference of the report, ie definitions, sources of information, methods used, limits, timing, layout or structure of the report and overall results. There may be mention of who authorised or commissioned the report.

In the **body** of a report, facts are presented.
• Headings are used to guide the reader through the report, and underlining, repetition or bold type are used to emphasise points.

• Sections begin with a topic sentence, or an expansion of the heading.
• Whenever a section contains two or more subsections, these tend to be numbered, eg 3.1, 3.2, etc and sub-headings are used.
• Sentences and paragraphs should be kept reasonably short.
• Visuals such as charts are used to clarify information.

There is no new information in the **final** or **terminal** section. Points are summarised (in the same order as in the report), conclusions are drawn, and action-driven recommendations are made.

2 A pharmaceutical company recently held a convention for doctors and other medical staff. You have been asked to analyse feedback on the convention.

Look at the graphs for this year and last year. Write an executive summary of no more than 250 words describing and analysing the results and suggest modifications for the future. Use the following outline.

Part 1: Background and purpose – two or three sentences indicating the purpose of the report and giving an overview of findings

Part 2: Presentation of the data – four sub-headings comparing and contrasting figures, with possible explanations for the data

Part 3: Conclusions and recommendations – summarise part 2, outline possible options, draw a conclusion and make a recommendation for the future

Customer satisfaction: this year

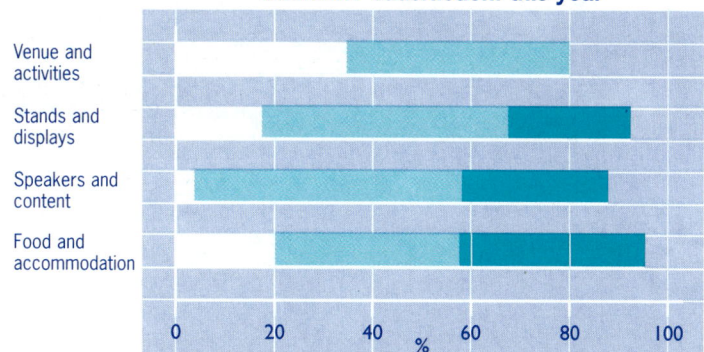

Venue and activities
Stands and displays
Speakers and content
Food and accommodation

0   20   40   %   60   80   100

Customer satisfaction: last year

Venue and activities
Stands and displays
Speakers and content
Food and accommodation

0   20   40   %   60   80   100

☐ very good   ■ good   ■ poor

Reading and listening

1 Look at extracts A–D below. They come from the contents page of a trade magazine.

For each of the following statements, choose one extract (A–D).

1 Not everybody can go to this event every day. ____

2 This is a service rather than an event and does not operate everywhere. ____

3 This fair is aimed at people wishing to become entrepreneurs. ____

4 This fair is new to the region. ____

5 This fair caters for smaller exhibitors. ____

A

PAGE 6

Beyond 2010   *April 2–8*

The latest in hi-tech in a hands-on environment. Promoters and product-seekers alike, now is the time to prepare yourself for this avant-garde fair, the first ever to be held on your home territory. All major hi-tech concerns will be present at the fair, a launching pad for ideas, systems and novelties. Smaller concerns will be in the same pavilions as the leaders and not set aside as a fringe show. A not-to-be-missed opportunity to move where the future is heading.

B

PAGE 9

Construction Trade Fair   *April 25–30*

For the first time this decade, an international fair on your very own doorstep. The best place to be represented and to find representatives in the leading technology in this sector. The fair includes a symposium on trends in the industry – both domestic and industrial – as well as a brand-new section on agricultural buildings. Days one and two for professionals only.

C

PAGE 11

International Franchising Fair   *March 12–16*

Interested in setting up shop without incurring all the normal risks? Interested in a safe investment? Want to meet experts in franchising? This fair will open doors for you! Companies with a proven track record and newcomers to this field will be present to convince you with their know-how, back-up and general expertise. A wide range of business opportunities to choose from, including fast-food restaurants, hotels and most retail sectors, as well as services such as accounting and tax advisory services, dental clinics, beauty parlours, play and learning centres.

D

PAGE 15

SOS Fairs and Exhibitions

Made-to-measure stands to suit your needs. SOS can provide the service you need in a selected range of venues, including attractive stands, interpreters and translators, pre-fair mailings, on-line publicity, access to promotional tools to suit local needs, cultural briefings, dealing with potential clients, etc. Prices to match your budget.

2 🎧 You will hear four extracts from conversations or presentations which relate to the fairs or services described in Exercise 1.

Match each extract to one of the fairs or services. Did the dialogues occur *before*, *after*, or *at* the fair?

1 _____

2 _____

3 _____

4 _____

3 🎧 You are going to hear Xavier Vidal, an export manager, talk about his job. He works for a small multinational manufacturer and distributor of water treatment products. Their clients range from fish-farmers to swimming pool builders. In the interview he describes how he prepares for trips abroad. He then talks about trade fairs, the way fairs vary from country to country and sector to sector, and what he thinks lies ahead.

Listen and choose the correct alternative to complete the sentences.

1 Primary information is gathered before going on a business trip _____.
   a) to get in touch with clients
   b) to find out about possible clients
   c) to find out more about established clients

2 A database of possible clients is set up _____.
   a) after making an appointment with them
   b) after information has been gathered via the internet, Yellow Pages and so on
   c) when introducing your company to them by fax

3 Fairs take up more time and energy in developing countries because _____.
   a) the visitors are not always businesspeople
   b) potential clients ask more things
   c) the fairs are multi-sector

4 In developing countries problems can arise because of _____.
   a) the difficulty involved in distinguishing roles clearly
   b) the absence of professionals
   c) the need for communication

5 The role of trade fairs is changing _____.
   a) because people are more communicative
   b) because the internet brings fairs to people
   c) because new products are already familiar to clients

6 Fairs in the future will be used to _____.
   a) consolidate and foster existing client relationships
   b) do market research
   c) take clients out to supper

C Speaking

Product presentations

Effective speakers use linguistic devices to attract and hold attention. Here are some useful techniques.

Repetition
It's comfortable. It's comfortable because it's well-designed, made of the best materials and very easy to use.

Rhetorical questions (asking questions and then answering them yourself)
How much does it cost? Much less than competing products.

Short answers
What's the situation regarding after-sales service? Excellent.

Tripling – groups of three adjectives, concepts, facts
The service is fast, safe and reliable.

1 Many sales people prepare a mini-presentation of their product before going to a trade fair. Very often company representatives learn them by heart. Doing so gives them confidence and visitors are often impressed by their fluency.

Look at the following presentation. What techniques mentioned in the speaking tips box above are used to sell the product?

I would like to show you our range of workstation furniture. Here on the left we have our latest designs in ergonomic desks. Why do we call them ergonomic? Because they adapt to the employee. Does that make a difference? Yes, it does. It means no bad backs, no aching wrists, no tired eyes. And that means fewer days off work. The desks are made of natural materials and are easy to install. They are adjustable, long-lasting and more reasonably priced than you may think. Now if you look closely …

2 Choose a product or a service to present in class.

1 Write down three positive features to describe the service or product, eg *innovative*.
2 Write down one rhetorical question you could use to attract interest, eg *Why do you need this service?*
3 Write down a short statement about the product/service to repeat, eg *This simple tool could change your life. This simple tool could change your life because it saves time.*

Prepare and then give a mini-presentation using the above techniques to sell your product/service. You will have to present your product at a fair. Beforehand, take time to practise your presentation so that you can give it with confidence.

The language of requests and offers

Before speaking, think about the following:
• How formal do I need to be? (What is the appropriate way to start?)
• What can I do to avoid sounding abrupt or rude? (Are there any linguistic forms that I should avoid?)
• Is my intonation and tone of voice appropriate? (Or do I unwittingly change appropriate utterances into rude-sounding ones?)

3 Look at the requests and offers below. Choose the most appropriate alternative(s) for each situation and discuss what you feel is wrong with the others. Suggest alternative ways of making the same requests and offers and practise saying them.

1 Requesting a catalogue
   a) Excuse me, could I possibly have a catalogue?
   b) A catalogue, please.
   c) Excuse me; give me a catalogue.

2 Requesting a price list
   a) I hope you don't mind my asking, but do you happen to have a price list?
   b) Excuse me, can I have a price list, please?
   c) Sorry, give me a price list, will you?

3 Requesting more information
   a) Could you send me some more information when you get back to your head office?
   b) Now, when you get back to head office, I want you to send me some more information.
   c) I would be very grateful if you would be kind enough to forward some more information at your earliest convenience.

4 Offering a catalogue
   a) Here's our catalogue.
   b) Here, take our catalogue, would you?
   c) Would you be so good as to take our catalogue?

5 Offering to send more information
   a) Would you like us to send some more information?
   b) We would be honoured to send you some more information, if that is your wish.
   c) Shall we send you some more information?

6 Offering to meet
   a) Shall we meet after lunch?
   b) I suggest we meet this afternoon.
   c) We would be delighted to have a meeting to discuss matters, if you can spare us the time. Would tomorrow suit you?

4 This role play is for two speakers.

You are both at a trade fair. A is visiting the fair, and B is working at a stand. A visits B's stand to find out about B's product. Before beginning, B should name the product or service he/she is selling and A should decide who he/she represents.

A looks at this page. B turns to page 77.

SPEAKER A

- Greet B.
- Ask for a catalogue.
- Ask about the product/service B is offering.
- Request a price list and some further information.
- Agree to B's suggestion of a meeting and suggest a day/time.

It's a cyber world

describing the uses of
computers and the internet

teleworking

writing e-mails

preparing short speeches

KEY VOCABULARY

Choose the correct definition to complete the following sentences.

1 An electronic point of sale system means _____.

2 A teleworker is _____.

3 Downloading means _____.

4 A portal is _____.

5 E-commerce means _____.

6 Groupware is _____.

a) a "supersite" in the world wide web that provides a range of services such as searching tools, news, e-mail, discussion groups and links to other sites
b) that tills or cash registers are connected to a computer which collects and processes data regarding sales and stocks
c) buying and selling through the internet (also called e-tailing or e-business; either B2B – business-to-business – or B2C – business-to-consumer)
d) software and systems designed to facilitate group communication, co-ordination and decision-making; used widely in intranets – internal computer networks
e) receiving a file through the internet or an internal network
f) someone who works not in an office but from home and is connected to the employer electronically

A Listening and writing

1 🎧 Listen to five reports from different business sectors about how information technology (IT) is applied and exploited in each sector. Identify the sector for each report.

1 ____	A building supplies
2 ____	B agriculture
3 ____	C retail fashion
4 ____	D office supplies
5 ____	E wholesale fashion
	F sports goods
	G banking
	H animal husbandry

2 Listen again and match each report with one of these summaries.

a) Consumer demands led to the application of new technology. ____

b) The company introduced a system to control loss of stock. ____

c) The company only uses IT to control stocks. ____

d) The company has an innovative IT feature which helps customers to make decisions about what to buy. ____

e) The reason for changing the IT system was to facilitate stock control and movement between stores. ____

f) IT systems have provided the company with information that has changed the way orders are made. ____

g) IT systems facilitate creativity. ____

h) The company only uses computers for bookkeeping. ____

3 The fashion wholesaler above, Ducatissimo, has written an e-mail to the retail fashion chainstore, Webster's, offering a limited range of items for the current season. Read the writing tips and the e-mail. Does the e-mail follow all the rules?

WRITING TIPS

E-mails

- E-mails tend to be less formal than other written business documents but more formal than conversational language. The degree of formality will depend on who the receiver is, and whether or not you have met the receiver. As a rule, formal terms such as *Yours faithfully/Yours sincerely* are replaced by *Regards/With best wishes*.
- Effective business e-mails should be brief, clear and action-driven.
- When replying to an e-mail, do not include the original e-mail if it is not necessary.
- Long documents (eg reports) are best sent as an attachment to a short covering note.
- Use the bcc (blind copy) feature when the e-mail is being sent to more than one person or company and you wish to keep that a secret.
- Make sure that the subject line is clear. With people receiving 70–100 e-mails a day, the most interesting-looking e-mails will be opened first.
- Screen sizes vary, so use a maximum of 72 characters per line.
- Do not overuse capital letters: they SHOUT.
- Always check spelling and grammar.

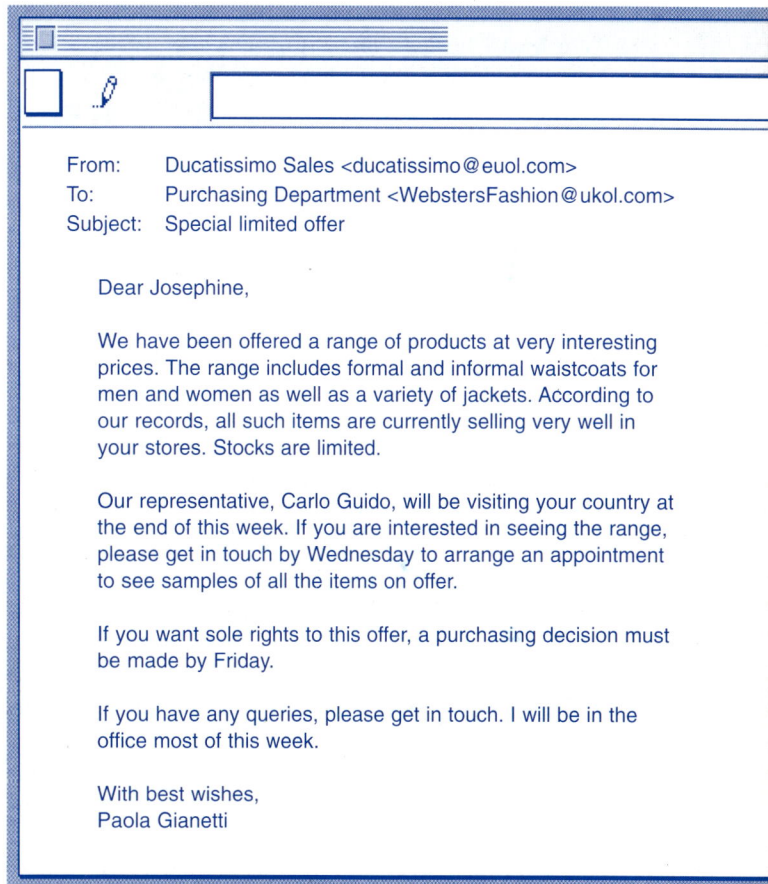

From: Ducatissimo Sales <ducatissimo@euol.com>
To: Purchasing Department <WebstersFashion@ukol.com>
Subject: Special limited offer

Dear Josephine,

We have been offered a range of products at very interesting prices. The range includes formal and informal waistcoats for men and women as well as a variety of jackets. According to our records, all such items are currently selling very well in your stores. Stocks are limited.

Our representative, Carlo Guido, will be visiting your country at the end of this week. If you are interested in seeing the range, please get in touch by Wednesday to arrange an appointment to see samples of all the items on offer.

If you want sole rights to this offer, a purchasing decision must be made by Friday.

If you have any queries, please get in touch. I will be in the office most of this week.

With best wishes,
Paola Gianetti

4 Read the following notes and write a reply of around 200 words.

You know that Ducatissimo occasionally imports surplus stocks from the southern hemisphere (especially Australia, Argentina, Brazil and Chile) to sell off the following season in the northern hemisphere (especially in the UK and Ireland). The products are often (but not always) a bargain and are worth looking at.

You can meet first thing Thursday in your office, or Friday morning at around 11. You need to know how long the meeting will take (you may need to shift other appointments). You want Carlo to be on time.

Mention your concern regarding:

- labels (English? Spanish? Portuguese?). They need to be in English. Can this be guaranteed?
- delivery (Easter OK; after mid-May – right to cancel?)
- sizes and quantities (are complete ranges available, or odd sizes?)

You also need further information on minimum quantities and discounts.

1 Read the article about the proliferation of telework and choose the correct alternative to fill each gap.

THE OPEN-COLLAR WORKER

At the end of the nineteenth century, nearly 90 per cent of North Americans were self-employed. Many worked from home, running farms or plying a trade in a garage or empty shed. Doctors visited patients in their homes, shop-owners lived behind or above their business. The twentieth-century industrial revolution gave rise to the transition from farms to factories. Now, the cyber revolution is bringing jobs and family back together.

Currently, the fastest-growing workforce is home-based. Many businesses and organisations are allowing and even encouraging employees to work from home. In 1975, only 2.5 million North Americans worked from home. Twenty-five years later, this figure had (1) _____ to over 50 million. In other words, an estimated 40 per cent of the workforce was working part- or full-time from home. Large companies like AT&T and IBM (2) _____ programmes that had allowed thousands of employees (36,000-odd in the case of AT&T) to combine home, mobile and in-office work styles. Smaller companies had also reengineered and set up telework systems. A Colorado-based groupware vendor decided to practise what they preached and their entire staff became teleworkers. The firm's headquarters are now in a smallish office used for meetings, get-togethers and customer demonstrations. (3)_____ the company says that their overheads have fallen 30 per cent, staff are more productive and morale is higher.

The advertisements for telework have become familiar: picture a large house with a swimming pool; at a table by the pool sits our teleworker with a laptop computer, cell phone and a case of files. No more traffic jams; no more clocking in; this is a technological revolution, this is a new way of life. Sociologists (4) _____ that the reality is often a far cry from this blissful scene. The majority of teleworkers or telecommuters (or "open-collar" workers as they are also called) do not spend their day working in a relaxed manner by the pool. (5) _____, the working conditions of open-collar workers are frequently far from optimal. Many have their home office (6) _____ in a bedroom or in a specially designed cupboard which opens out into a pseudo-office.

Open-collar workers are often more productive at the expense of working long hours. They can become workaholics, frequently putting in 60 to 80 hours a week. Many do not take holidays (7) _____ of missing out on that "big job".

Loneliness and a lack of self-pride are two other factors psychologists say affect the open-collar worker. The absence of daily interaction with colleagues produces a feeling of isolation. The need to adhere to office dress codes is no longer there and (8) _____ this seems liberating initially, working in pyjamas all day long can be dangerous from the psychological point of view (and not only because a client or supervisor might turn up unexpectedly on your doorstep). Psychologists and sociologists seem to agree that the open-collar worker needs to plan and prioritise so as not to fall into the pitfalls of this type of employment. First and (9) _____, one should see telework as a job, not a lifestyle. Secondly, one needs to build in self-discipline – a fixed time for lunch, breaks from the screen and so on (10) _____ than spontaneous visits to the refrigerator and too much television. Thirdly, one should fight off isolation by joining professional bodies, attending workshops and keeping in touch with colleagues.

1 a) got	b) flown	c) soared	d) raised
2 a) had developed	b) developed	c) had done	d) have done
3 a) As a result	b) On the contrary	c) Otherwise	d) However
4 a) point to	b) point out	c) underline	d) repeat over
5 a) Mostly	b) Above all	c) Although	d) Indeed
6 a) setting up	b) set up	c) arranged	d) arranging
7 a) because	b) worried	c) anxious	d) for fear
8 a) meanwhile	b) as	c) whilst	d) because
9 a) foremost	b) overall	c) for all	d) best
10 a) more	b) less	c) rather	d) instead

2 Work in pairs. Write down the advantages and drawbacks of working from home that are mentioned in the text. What other points can you think of?

3 The weekend magazine of a widely read newspaper published a pullout
   supplement on e-commerce, teleworking and the internet. Part of the contents
   page has been reproduced below. Look at the summary sentences 1–6 below and
   match them to extracts A–D.

   1 This article gives advice to companies considering e-commerce. ____

   2 This article probably talks about how you can protect yourself from internet
      fraud. ____

   3 You'll be interested in this article if you want to make a good impression in
      public. ____

   4 If you want an overview of the latest on the world wide web, start here. ____

   5 For a comparison of search engines, read this article. ____

   6 This article talks about your legal rights. ____

A

E-commerce? It's not safe!

PAGE

Trust and security are two factors which inhibit people from buying and selling on-line.
How safe is it to enter your credit card number into the net? How much can hackers
find out? How does one file a claim for products that arrive damaged or are of inferior
quality? How is consumer protection ensured? What is the current legal situation
regarding e-commerce?

Your queries are answered by our legal advisors ...

5

B

"A speech on-line is a speech in time"

You're under pressure, you've got a major event coming up and YOU have been chosen
to give the welcoming speech! Your company has just tied up a major contract and there
is a dinner to celebrate – who's going to write the main speech, yet alone deliver it?

Speeches for births, deaths and marriages, to accompany the golden handshake or the
annual convention. You name it, you can get it – in time, on-line; tailor-made or off-the-
shelf. Available since the mid-1990s, this site receives around 1,000 hits a day. How
much money and work is involved? Regular upgrading of the site and ensuring entry
into search engines are significant ongoing costs in the business. But business is
booming ... Who is behind it and how does it work?

9

C

What's for sale?

An update on most goods and services you can buy or access on-line (software,
educational and training products, music and multimedia, publications, electronics,
banking, pharmaceuticals, airline tickets, stock and mutual funds, advice of all types,
household products and so on). New additions are highlighted, reliable search engines
and interesting trends pointed out, and there's hot-off-the-press news and rumours
about future developments ... In short, your Yellow Pages hit list ...

11

D

Setting up shop on the net?

At long last, after being bombarded with so much talk and pressure about e-commerce
(how if you're not in you'll be out, that e-commerce is growing at a spectacular rate, etc)
you've decided to give it a go. But where should you begin? How much does it cost to
start up? What's the difference between B2B and B2C? What overheads will you incur?
Is it really worth it?

A detailed analysis of the pros and cons of e-commerce for the smaller and mid-sized
company. A questionnaire to help you on your way and a survey of what's on offer and
at what price.

14

---

4 Work in pairs. Write down three sentences similar to the ones in Exercise 3 above
   and ask your partner to identify the extract referred to.

5 Which articles are targeted at   a) businesses?   b) individuals?   c) both?

C Speaking

1 Work on your own first, then compare your views in pairs or threes.

The Global Management Institute is a business school for executives. Recently, participants on a course entitled "Speaking in Public" received the following list of points to bear in mind when speaking in public.

1 Decide which of the points you can prepare in advance.
2 How important is each point? How might each one affect the delivery of a talk? Give reasons.
3 Discuss other factors you consider important.

SPEAKING IN PUBLIC

Check your diction and pronunciation of key words.

Introduce no more than seven main ideas.

Memorise the beginning and the end of the talk.

Mention the aim or purpose of your talk.

Give an outline of your talk.

Practise fixing your eyes on two points in the audience.

Practise the talk several times if you can.

Repeat or paraphrase key points.

Summarise the key ideas towards the end.

Time yourself.

Use mostly simple, short sentences.

Write key ideas in CAPITAL LETTERS in the margin or on prompt cards.

2 The following is a list of ways to attract the attention of your audience right at the beginning of your talk. Match them with the talk openings A–E below.

1 Facts and figures ____
2 Anecdote/story/joke ____
3 Formal greeting ____
4 Quote ____
5 Rhetorical question(s) ____

A Good evening, ladies and gentlemen, and thank you for inviting me here this evening to talk about e-commerce and its effect on retailing and consumer behaviour. I'm going to describe and analyse recent research carried out in the field and then give my own vision of what is to come.

B Three friends, a chemist, a physicist and an IT expert, were going up a hill in a car when the car broke down. They discussed the problem. The chemist said, "I think that change of oil is the problem. The octane level may not have been right." The physicist said, "I think we must have changed into the wrong gear halfway up the hill." The IT expert said, "I don't know what the cause of the problem is, but I'm pretty sure that if we turn the car off, all get out, and then get back in again and turn the car back on, it'll run again."

C Can you remember what life was like before e-mail?

D   This time last year we had just started out and we had 4,000 clients in all. During the course of this evening we're likely to gain 4,000 new clients, willing to pay 100 euros per annum for our services.

E   At the turn of the millennium, in a conference in Madrid, Spain, Bill Gates, the founder of Microsoft, said, "We must ensure that technology reaches the developing nations: without it, they will get nowhere."

3   Discuss the following in pairs or small groups.

1   Which of the above openings would you feel happy using?
2   Think of examples of other facts, anecdotes, formal greetings, jokes, quotes, and rhetorical questions you could use.
3   Can you think of other ways to begin a speech?

4   🎧 Listen to a Brazilian website designer, Lilian Varela, giving a short speech on the characteristics of a good website as part of her English examination.

1   How long is the speech?
2   How does she start?
3   Does she give an outline of what she is going to say?
4   Does she summarise at the end?
5   Which of the points below does she mention and in what order?
    a) content
    b) easy to use
    c) frequent updating
    d) purchasing possibilities
    e) downloading time

5   Choose one of the following topics. Use the space below to brainstorm and make notes about what you want to say. Take two minutes to do this, decide how to begin and then speak to the class for one and a half minutes. When you have finished, invite your audience to make comments and/or ask questions.

1   The best websites I've visited
2   The importance of a website for a company's image
3   The effect e-commerce will have on consumer behaviour and retailing
4   The future of e-commerce in different parts of the world
5   Products and services that could never be sold on-line
6   The advantages and disadvantages of e-mail

Topic no:

Opening:

Points:

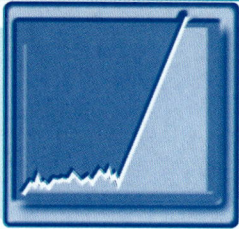

bank loans

raising capital

presenting and comparing
investment opportunities

persuading people

UNIT 5

Investment and growth

KEY VOCABULARY

Combine words from the two columns below to make word pairs/partners,
eg *treasury + bonds = treasury bonds*.

A	B
bear	account
bull	bonds
current	loan
long-term	market
pension	plan
stock	
short-term	
treasury	

Use the combinations to complete the following definitions. The first one has been
done for you.

1   <u>Treasury bonds</u> (also called **government bonds** and **gilt-edged stocks**):
an investment underwritten by the government. Interest is paid at regular
intervals and the lump sum invested is returned at the end of a given period,
eg ten years.

2   _____: money borrowed for a short period of time, normally
at a fixed rate of interest.

3   _____: money borrowed for a long period of time, eg a
mortgage. The interest rate may be fixed or variable.

4   _____ (or **exchange**): the place where stocks (fixed-interest
securities) and shares in companies are bought and sold.

5   _____: a term used to refer to a downturn in the value of
stocks and shares (when the resale value is lower than the purchase price).
The opposite is a _____, when the resale value is higher and
capital gain, ie a profit, can be made.

6   _____: a bank deposit which allows the company or
individual to withdraw money at any time.

7   _____: a scheme whereby money is deposited regularly over
many years in return for a fixed income upon reaching retirement.

A   Listening

1   ⧉ In a bank, risk analysts are responsible for examining the risk involved in
applications for loans, mortgages and credit facilities and deciding whether to
approve the application or not. Listen to risk analysts describing cases in which
loans were or were not granted. In each case, decide whether the loan was
approved (✓) or denied (✗).

1 ____   2 ____   3 ____   4 ____   5 ____

2 Now match each case (1–5) with the statements below. For one case there are two statements.

a) The applicant's total income did not appear to be declared officially. ____

b) The company was solvent. ____

c) The loan was applied for at the last minute. ____

d) The ownership of the company had changed. ____

e) There had been an inspection of the company recently. ____

f) This company was apparently not very solvent. ____

3 Discuss whether you would request a bank loan:

- to buy an expensive car
- to pay a tax return
- to buy shares on the stock exchange

4 🎧 Listen to an investor, J.C., describing his personal approach to investment, and choose the correct alternative to complete the sentences.

1 J.C. started investing in shares _____.
   a) to receive an annual yield on his investments
   b) to make a profit quickly
   c) for the same reason as he invested in pension plans

2 Large-scale privatisation of companies in the United Kingdom _____.
   a) enabled people to make large amounts of money
   b) started after privatisation in other European countries
   c) is only a trend

3 People lost interest in receiving dividends on their shares because _____.
   a) the resale value mattered more
   b) there were no dividends being paid
   c) their shares were privatised

4 Before investing in the stock exchange you should _____.
   a) decide whether or not you can handle losses
   b) see if it will hurt you
   c) decide whether or not you like bull markets

5 Black Monday was on _____ and the New York stock exchange _____.
   a) October 19, 1987; fell to 25 points
   b) October 9, 1987; went down 25 per cent
   c) October 19, 1987; fell 25 per cent

6 Black Monday did not affect people who _____.
   a) needed the money immediately and had to sell their shares
   b) sell whenever there is a bull market
   c) were patient and did not sell at the time

7 If there is a downturn in the stock market, _____.
   a) most people will be prepared for it
   b) many people will not know how to react
   c) most investors will have to sell all their shares

8 Risk profile refers to _____.
   a) the amount of money you invest in the stock exchange
   b) the amount you are willing to invest without being concerned about gains and losses
   c) the amount of money you can afford to lose daily

5 What is your own risk profile? Discuss and give examples.

1 Read the following article about the origins of the Hard Rock Cafe, and choose the correct alternative to fill each gap.

"Rock Around the Clock Tonight"

Back in 1970 a young man, Isaac Tigrett, decided that London was well and truly ready and possibly even dying for American-style food – hamburgers, chicken and ribs. (1) _____, as he had never run a restaurant, he took on a (2) _____, another American, Peter Morton, who at the time was running a restaurant called The Great American Disaster. Each of them put up $5,000; they (3) _____ a further $35,000 from a bank in Europe and in June 1971 the first Hard Rock Cafe was opened.

The restaurant was an instant success, with (4) _____ customers lining up, waiting to get in. Famous celebrities could be seen there and T-shirts and sweatshirts with the Hard Rock emblem (5) _____ the "in" thing to buy for oneself and friends alike.

In 1982, Tigrett and Morton decided to (6) _____ the partnership. The deal they finally struck was complex. On the one hand, Morton retained the rights to operate Hard Rock Cafes in the USA west of the Mississippi River, except for Texas (but with Houston) and also in Illinois and Louisiana. He also got rights for a number of countries: Brazil, Venezuela, Israel, Australia and parts of Canada, and a (7) _____ sum of $800,000 for his (8) _____ in the London restaurant. Tigrett, on the other hand, got the London restaurant and set-up rights for the rest of the world.

Morton soon opened highly successful (9) _____ of the Hard Rock Cafe in San Francisco, Los Angeles and Chicago. Tigrett went to the cities of Stockholm, Reykjavik and New York. Tigrett adopted a "think big" strategy. It cost $3.6 million to set up in New York, largely (10) _____ the decor. In order to (11) _____ this investment and attract crowds at the same time, Tigrett took on two very influential partners – Yul Brynner and Dan Aykroyd. The business proved very (12) _____. In 1984, restaurant (13) _____ were $7 million. The profit (14) _____ was a very healthy 17 per cent ($1.2 million) and well above the (15) _____ (4.2 per cent) for the sector.

1 a) Although	b) However	c) Nevertheless	d) So
2 a) partner	b) person	c) colleague	d) investor
3 a) received	b) lent	c) borrowed	d) required
4 a) first	b) all	c) would-be	d) model
5 a) became	b) becoming	c) was	d) being
6 a) end up	b) conclude	c) stop	d) dissolve
7 a) lump	b) fixed	c) negotiated	d) payout
8 a) portion	b) share	c) proportion	d) staking
9 a) sections	b) reproductions	c) branches	d) set-ups
10 a) because	b) because of	c) for	d) due

11 a) reduce   b) pay   c) finance   d) redeem
12 a) acquisitive b) beneficial c) gainful   d) profitable
13 a) takings   b) turnover   c) incomes   d) profits
14 a) earnings   b) and loss   c) margin   d) accrued
15 a) usual   b) accepted   c) medium   d) average

2 Morton and Tigrett obtained start-up or seed capital from a European bank. Tigrett took on partners to finance the growth of his Hard Rock Cafe business. In what other ways can the expansion of a business be financed?

3 Polansquimi manufactures medicines mainly for the veterinary market. The demand for Polansquimi's products has grown, the current plant is reaching its maximum capacity and the company wants to branch out into a new area of products. They will therefore have to relocate to an industrial estate and build a new factory. This represents a major investment.

Read the text below. It comes from an accountant's report outlining ways to finance the above investment. In each numbered line (1–10) there is one wrong word. Underline the word and write the correct word in the space. The first one has been done as an example.

Investigations show that despite the profitability of their investment, which has been paying out handsome dividends for many years, most of the original shareholders would be unwilling to subscribe for further shares in a new issue.

New Partners

1 Our research shows that a significant amount of capital could be <u>risen</u> from   *raised*

2 some of the company's larger supplies, who would be willing to acquire a stake   _____

3 in the company. These would mean no financial risk for the current owners.   _____

4 Partnership conditions would have to be negotiated so safeguard the   _____

5 independents of the present management team.   _____

Private Investors

6 A number of possible investments have been sounded out. Some would be able to   _____

7 finance the entire venture. Much investors demand part-ownership of the company   _____

8 and a right to take certain decisions in return for assuming the entirely risk. If the _____

9 growth plan meets expectations, additional capital would be done available. The   _____

10 company will need to supply potential investors with a excellent and well-documented business plan.   _____

Merchant Bank

Most merchant or investment banks would be able and perhaps even eager to invest in the company. However, these banks are currently imposing conditions which merit detailed examination.

4 What part of a report is this? Which of the alternative(s) does the accountant seem to favour? How do you know?

C Speaking and writing

The language of discussion and persuasion

When trying to convince somebody about something, we must first of all sound convincing. It is not always necessary to raise your voice. Calm, collected, firm speech can be more effective than a forceful, vehement tone of voice.

A variety of set phrases will also help you to sound more convincing:

Promoting with enthusiasm
This venture is a sound investment. This is a company with a proven track record and a great future.
This is a unique opportunity to invest money in an exciting project.

Comparing the option with others
This venture involves much less risk than the others do.
This venture requires a lot more capital than the others do.

Predicting results
In three years' time this will be making larger profits than the others will.
If you invest in The Olive Shop, you will get an estimated annual return of 15 per cent.

Inviting agreement
Don't you think this idea has great potential?
Wouldn't you agree that this is a unique opportunity?

Agreeing
I think you're absolutely right.
That's a great idea!

Disagreeing
I'm not sure I agree with you.
I don't see it like that.

Partly agreeing
I partly agree with what you're saying.
I agree to some extent.

Think of one other expression for at least three categories.

1 This role play is for four speakers. You have received inside information about a promising investment. Each of you has information about a different company.

    1 Work on your own. Prepare to give a mini-presentation of your company (see role play cards on pages 33 and 77). Decide why you would or should invest in the company. Then plan how to begin your presentation of the company (eg _____ *is an attractive investment from all points of view*) and how to convince your partners of the viability of your venture.

    2 Work together. Give mini-presentations of your ventures to each other. Ask questions if you wish.

    3 Work on your own. Score each of the ventures from 1–4 (1 = most appealing option) and note down a reason for your decision.

    4 Work together. Compare notes with other group members and discuss the options in terms of the following:

- initial capital investment
- running costs
- job creation
- profitability
- risk/likelihood of succeeding

5   Discuss which two ventures you think will be most successful, and which, if any, might fail and why.

A looks at this page. B turns to page 77. C turns to page 77. D turns to page 77.

SPEAKER A

Business start-up: Penguin Park

A tourist attraction with real penguins of all types in their natural habitat. Monorail yourself into the frozen world of the Antarctic and observe Emperor and King Penguins. Exhilarating rides like The Penguin Splash, carousels, side-shows, hands-on blue penguins and panoramic cinema form part of a breathtaking itinerary.

Initial investment: 30,000,000 euros
Projected income: 15,000,000 euros p.a.
Projected expenditure: 8,000,000 euros p.a.
Jobs: 100
Breakeven: five years

2   You have decided to approach a venture capitalist to raise finance for one of the ventures in Exercise 1. Write the covering letter to accompany a detailed business plan.

Before you start, organise your thoughts. A potential business partner will be looking for clear, well-thought-out ideas.

With your neighbour, briefly discuss:

- whether or not to include all the points mentioned in the box below
- if there are other points that should be mentioned

- mention your previous experience
- mention your qualifications and skills
- outline the project
- refer to the business plan
- refer to the profitability of the venture
- refer to your personal attributes
- request an appointment to discuss the matter
- state why you have chosen to approach this particular venture capitalist

Now discuss how to organise the content:

- How are you going to begin? (Are you going to refer to the project? refer to why you have chosen to approach the reader? refer to someone who has made a recommendation? etc)
- What *else* are you going to say in the opening?
- What is the best order to list points in the body of the letter?
- How are you going to end the letter?

Write the letter. How long did it take you?

production and
the environment

accidents

occupational health

describing processes

Is it safe?

KEY VOCABULARY

BIOLOGICAL DIVERSITY – the full range of living organisms occurring in nature

ENVIRONMENTAL IMPACT – the effect that human activity (eg a manufacturing process) can have on nature

ERGONOMICS – the study of the physical and environmental conditions of work. An ergonomic audit details aspects that can be improved.

GENETICALLY MODIFIED – refers to an animal or vegetable whose genes have been altered so as to resist disease, climatic conditions, etc

OCCUPATIONAL HEALTH – the area of medicine dealing with the prevention and treatment of work-related injuries and illnesses

A

Listening

1 🎧 Listen to part of an interview with Svend Auken, a Danish politician, about the relationship between the globalisation of economies and environmental impact. Choose the correct alternative to complete the sentences.

1 Consumers are worried mainly about _____.
   a) information, standards and labelling
   b) international trade agreements
   c) regulations being too strict

2 The United States and the European Union _____.
   a) agree about genetically modified food
   b) agree about the labelling of genetically modified food
   c) disagree about the labelling of genetically modified food

3 Prior to the creation of an open internal market within the European Union,

   _____.
   a) most countries had tight environmental policies
   b) standards and regulations varied from country to country
   c) the quality of life of European citizens was not guaranteed

4 Europe's desire to harmonise standards and regulations regarding health,

   safety and the environment _____.
   a) has been welcomed by the United States
   b) is another way of setting up trade barriers
   c) is sometimes seen as a means to set up trade barriers

5 The cost of the environmental impact of transportation _____.
   a) is fully paid for by taxes and other charges
   b) is not a real cost
   c) is covered in some cases at a national level

6 Auken's view of what lies ahead is that _____.
   a) the future is grim
   b) future changes are inevitable
   c) the West is short-sighted

2 🎧 Listen to Tom Dwyer, author of the book *Life and Death at Work*, outlining what he sees as key factors in industrial accidents. Complete the summary below using a number or up to three words for each gap.

Plenum Studies in Work and Industry

LIFE AND DEATH
AT WORK
*Industrial Accidents
as a Case of
Socially Produced Error*

TOM DWYER

Industrial accidents occur ___*at three*___ levels: organisation, command and reward.

Organisation-level Accidents

The Three Mile Island nuclear accident occurred because the way in which systems were interlinked was so complex that when things started going wrong, (1) _____ could not work out what the problem was.

(2) _____ must be built so that they can be understood intuitively.

Accidents occur on (3) _____ because of disorganisation and/or the absence of preventive measures like (4) _____.

(5) _____ reduces the incidence of accidents caused by monotonous, routine tasks.

Command-level Accidents

The nuclear accident at Chernobyl occurred because (6) _____ carried out during the night shift rather than the day shift. At night the supervisors in charge did not have enough authority to say "no" to the (7) _____. The latter group then ordered everyone about and their tests turned into disaster. Accidents can also be caused through (8) _____ communication in work groups. This cause alone accounts for approximately (9) _____ of all accidents. Sometimes these accidents happen because workers (10) _____.

Reward-level Accidents

When people are paid more if they produce more or work longer hours, they often end up endangering their lives. There is a larger number of accidents among those who work (11) _____ hours a day than among those working eight hours. The long working day of (12) _____, for example, can result in road accidents.

3 What would you do? Ask each other three of the following questions.

1 If you discovered that your favourite restaurant was employing illegal immigrant workers and paying them under the minimum rates for extremely long hours, would you stop going there to eat?
2 Would you buy shoes if you thought they had been made by young children?
3 There is a boycott of all goods coming from the country where one of your favourite toiletries is made. Do you continue to buy the product regardless?
4 If at work you were asked to do something that looked dangerous (eg climbing up an unsafe ladder to get down some heavy files), would you do it?
5 You have a highly infectious virus, but there's an important meeting programmed, and for a number of reasons, you're worried about your job. Do you go to work?
6 You are visiting what is to be your new office and factory. You only want to go in for a minute. Do you put on a safety helmet?
7 You have recently seen a documentary which described how your favourite drink was contaminated in the manufacturing process. Do you continue to buy the drink?

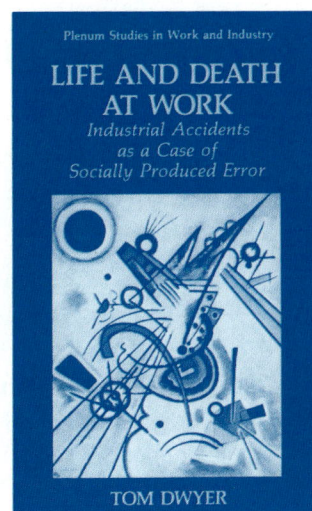

1 Many countries have decided to tackle the problem of occupational health. One such country is the Republic of Ireland. Look at the information about what a variety of organisations are doing to improve the situation. For each of the sentences on page 37, write the letter of one of the organisations.

A
HSA: Health & Safety Authority

A government body that enforces regulations and promotes health and safety in the workplace. Set up in 1989, the main aims and functions of the body are:
- to maintain a preventive attitude and approach to accidents;
- to foster and secure the safety, health and welfare of people at work;
- to encourage consultation between employers and employees everywhere.

The HSA gives information and advice to interested parties. In response to increased fatalities in the agricultural sector, for instance, they published a farm safety handbook. They regularly inspect premises and monitor compliance with health and safety regulations, and occasionally they carry out unannounced safety inspections.

B
The National Institute of Occupational Health

A private company specialising in occupational medicine, health supervision, occupational therapy and disability management. Ergonomic audits are carried out to determine the risk involved in production processes and alternatives are investigated so as to lower risk. When dealing with injured employees, rehabilitation is programmed to ensure that the employee returns to work at an optimal time and recovery level. In other words, recovery is managed so as to avoid relapses.

D
Occupational Healthworks is an organisation that works above all in the healthcare and aviation industries. They are specialists in minimising risk and treating illness. When carrying out an audit of a company's risk levels, Occupational Healthworks and the client's own health and safety personnel work side by side. In this way health hazards and safety risks are recognised jointly, awareness-building as to the legal requirements is ensured and, as a result, risk is minimised from the bottom up.

E
The Construction Industry Federation (CIF) is particularly affected by occupational accidents. Falls are the major cause of accidents, especially in the sub-areas of scaffolding and roof work. The federation now employs seven people full-time in a safety, environmental and training services unit. This unit offers members of the federation a group safety management scheme, safety audits and training courses. Its 30-hour course entitled Managing Safety in Construction is internationally recognised, and refresher courses have been created in response to demand. Safety induction courses for new employees are also run. Guidelines on safety management and on developing a safety statement have been published and the CIF's SCOPE programme (code of practice for scaffolding) is being used across Ireland.

C
The National Industrial Safety Organisation is a non-government organisation (NGO). In other words it is a voluntary body classified as a charity whose aim it is to promote occupational health and safety. Run by representatives of a wide range of organisations, including trade unions and insurance companies, it has identified and prioritised sectors that warrant special attention (eg the construction industry, the home). Activities include training courses, conferences, videos, posters, etc aimed at raising awareness, an annual safety quiz and the recognition of companies with positive occupational health practice through the NISO annual safety award. An increasing interest in this field is predicted as occupational stress-related illnesses rise.

1 This group works in close collaboration with its clients. ____

2 This group has legal authority. ____

3 This body focuses on one sector. ____

4 This body pinpoints industries that need advice. ____

5 One of the major functions of this organisation is to ensure that employees do not return to work too soon. ____

6 This body works mainly in two sectors. ____

7 This organisation gives a prize to companies that are safety-conscious. ____

8 The impact of the work of this body has attracted attention from other countries. ____

2 Read the text below. It is part of the introduction to a report. The report has been prepared by a company which is considering employing a team of specialists to reduce accident and sickness rates in the company. For each gap (1–10), write one appropriate word.

Concern has been expressed at various levels in our company at the rate of absenteeism (1) _____ to injury and ill health in our company, which is well above the industry average. Accidents can be caused by the lack of appropriate protective clothing such as helmets and safety glasses, as well as by other factors. The Employers' Federation has suggested that we have an ergonomic audit to ascertain the causes and apply solutions.

Ergonomics is a science (2) _____ is concerned with physical and environmental conditions of work and (3) _____ these conditions can be improved. Ergonomists study how people do their work. In other words, they analyse the physical relationship (4) _____ a person and the machine or tool he or she is working with, the movements and body position used, the design and layout of an office or work station, the lighting and environmental conditions, and so on. (5) _____ designing solutions, the underlying idea is to fit the job to the person (6) _____ than the person to the job. Good design, achieved (7) _____ the application of ergonomics, enhances the safety of tools, machines, job tasks and the working environment. (8) _____ only does this lead to a reduction in the number of work-related accidents, it also (9) _____ in better worker health, improved worker morale, increased efficiency and (10) _____ productivity on the job.

The report that follows examines why we need to employ a team of ergonomists, describes in detail the options available and assesses the long-term implications for the company. The report concludes that substantial improvements can be made in terms of productivity, staff morale and estimated long-term savings.

C Speaking and writing

GLOSSARY

CONVEYOR BELT – endless belt used in manufacture to move elements from one workstation to another

MUSCULOSKELETAL DISORDER – a medical complaint arising from poor body posture or repetitive strain injury (RSI) eg wrist/back strain; also called occupational overuse syndrome (OOS)

OVERHEAD BINS – raised, suspended containers, often connected to a conveyor belt, in or from which employees place or take items

SICK LEAVE – time taken off work because of injury or ill health

1 Le Chef is a catering company which serves a number of businesses and institutions. Recently, Le Chef has been having problems. Clients have reported sickness among their staff after eating meals Le Chef has supplied. Le Chef itself has a high rate of medical claims made by its employees. Health inspectors have been sent to investigate.

Work in pairs. Look at the inspector's notes together. Take it in turns to explain to your partner what questions were asked and/or details examined and what the findings were. The first one has been done for you.

Example: (1a) *We asked if the company had a safety officer. We found that she had left six months ago and had not been replaced. As a result no one is currently responsible for health and safety.*

Inspector: _____   **Date:** __ /__ /___

Comments

✓ satisfactory ✗ requires action

1. Administration

a. Is the safety committee/officer functional?	✗	left 6 months ago, not replaced
b. Do the staff receive regular retraining?	✗	nothing since safety officer left
c. Are crisis management procedures familiar to all?	✗	yes, but not revised for 5 years

2. Environment

a. Are the kitchens tidy, clean and well kept?	✗	first impression positive, close examination – bacteria, dirt in corners
b. Are the kitchens well ventilated?	✗	extractors poorly maintained
c. Is the temperature correct in all areas?	✗	uneven, too hot or too cold

3. Accident prevention

a. Do all cutting machines have a guard?	✗	some guards removed because loose
b. Do all staff wear the necessary protective clothing?	✗	clothing very old with holes and stains
c. Are hazardous areas clearly recognisable?	✓	correctly signed

4. Cleaning and sanitising

a. Are all cooking utensils cleaned properly?	✓	
b. Are the floors, walls and ceilings in good repair?	✗	cracks, peeling paint
c. Are the floors, walls, benches and other fittings clean?	✗	residual bacteria in cracks, signs of presence of beetles/mice

5. Workstations

a. Are the workstations designed so that utensils can be taken without stretching and twisting?	✗	poorly designed, some cupboards and racks have unsafe fixtures
b. Are forearms approximately parallel to the ground when working?	✗	rarely, excessive bending, tables too low

2 This pair work activity is for two speakers.

An international convention is being held to look at occupational health and safety. You have been sent to the convention to present a case study, in which the advice of ergonomists contributed to significant improvements in occupational health and substantial savings for your company. You will have to speak for a minute or two. In the presentation you will be expected to name/describe:

- the industry or sector
- the problem and how it was diagnosed
- the measures taken
- the results and any future plans

You may want to start like this:

Ladies and gentlemen, I am here today to describe the impact that a study by a group of ergonomists has had on our company, its productivity, staff morale and our future. We knew that there was an unusually high incidence of absenteeism related to illness. What we didn't know was the effect preventive measures could and would have.

A looks at this page. B turns to page 78. Present your case studies to each other.

SPEAKER A

CASE STUDY

Background: a high incidence of musculoskeletal injury rates and production problems in the mailroom of a large utilities company

Solutions: workstations rearranged, overhead bins lowered, wrist rests supplied, training to improve body posture

Results:
- productivity per worker up
- 1,200 fewer overtime hours/month (x 150% base wage rate)
- customers paid bills on average 1–2 days earlier (= 40,000 euros per day increased revenue from interest)
- average absenteeism fell from 1,010 to 584 hours/month

Future plans: ergonomic audits in other sectors, eg customer services

3 How important are health and safety at work? Talk to each other about the health and safety risks in your own jobs or in jobs you are familiar with. Which job has the highest risks?

4 Use the following guidelines to write a progress report on one of the cases you worked on in Exercise 2. The report should be in the form of a memo addressed to the Board of Directors.

- opening line: *The purpose of this report is to ...*
- background (explain why consultants were called in or how they analysed the problems)
- measures taken to date
- findings (illustrate with a graph/diagram if you wish)
- plans and proposals
- summary (one or two sentences)

It's a deal

suggesting and requesting

arguing and hypothesising

negotiating

KEY CONCEPTS

Work with your neighbour. To which group do you belong? What cultures do you identify with these characteristics?

- a **communitarian culture** in which individuals work for consensus and in the interests of the group or community
- an **individualist culture** in which individual freedom and responsibility are encouraged above all else
- a culture in which feelings are expressed openly
- a culture in which feelings are played down and subdued
- a culture in which bargaining is an everyday event
- a culture in which bargaining is relatively rare

A   Reading

1   Read the text below about approaches to negotiating. Choose the best sentence from a–i on page 41 to fill each gap.

─Trends in Negotiating Styles─

Bargaining between individuals and groups of individuals has gone on for centuries. Negotiating is often highly technical but it is also very much a human matter, involving personalities. People have their strengths and weaknesses, so a good deal of psychology is involved. (1) _____ They possess the power of analysis and can interpret the full meaning of what is being said and not said and how it is being said. They know how to stay calm and navigate their way through stormy negotiations. They have the patience to listen. They will allow and even encourage the other party to talk freely; in this way, information is obtained without the other party feeling threatened. Skilful negotiators will not display signs of victory or defeat and if the other party does have to retreat on a point, they will ensure that this can be done with grace. Even the most experienced negotiators cannot always avoid showdowns, ultimatums and deadlocks. (2) _____ After all, a solid business relationship is not only about money. The quality of interpersonal relations – the building of trust and rapport – can also make or break negotiations, and in some countries more than in others.

Negotiations must be prepared beforehand. If the company that is buying knows that there are alternative suppliers, then that information puts the buyer in a strong bargaining position. Similarly, if the seller knows that the buyer has few or no alternatives, then the seller is at a distinct advantage. (3) _____ Preparation for purchasing, for example, involves collecting data about the other party while analysing the company's own needs (price, time frame, technical specifications, and so on). (4) _____ Are prices as high as the market can take or are they kept low to ward off the competition? Or are prices merely based on getting a set rate of return on investment? Information of this nature lets the negotiator know the issues involved and how much flexibility there is.

Many books and films describe a sole negotiator, who after in-company discussions, goes to the negotiating table with a set of guidelines and takes decisions on the company's behalf. The objective is to reach an agreement, to make a deal quickly. (5) _____ The team will probably include professionals like a lawyer, an engineer or an economist.

Recently it has been pointed out that much of the above description is really only valid for individualist cultures like the United States and some northern European countries. In contrast, in communitarian cultures, like Singapore, Nigeria, Japan and France, negotiations take much longer than in individualist cultures. People regard achievement as being a team effort, so group rather than individual responsibility is assumed. (6) _____ This takes time but later often pays off.

In Japan, negotiations are subject to the "ringi" process. Those who go to the negotiating table are not necessarily those who later take the decisions. (7) _____ This then circulates amongst those who have the power to decide. Those who agree with the proposal presented to them initial it. That is how the final decision is made. In such countries people rarely go to the negotiating table alone and indeed in countries like Thailand, doing business surrounded by helpers is synonymous with high status. To arrive at a negotiating table unaccompanied may result in your status being seriously underestimated.

Thus when preparing for negotiations with businesspeople from a different culture, understanding how that other culture works may be as important to a successful outcome as research regarding prices and conditions.

a) Good negotiators are described as being quick, clear thinkers who express themselves articulately.

b) It is clear, therefore, that not all countries are the same.

c) Decisions are often referred back to the organisation, as all those concerned need to be consulted about the details.

d) If there is a team, members will have been fully briefed and are there to iron out legal and technical details.

e) The negotiator will be looking for data related to market share, current orders, the manufacturing process, and the fixing of prices.

f) They are there to gather information, to work out the details of a proposal.

g) If these occur prematurely, though, the result may be the end of the negotiations altogether.

h) In other words, one's own bargaining position and the bargaining strength of the other party must be analysed beforehand.

i) Status may also be defined by age, gender and social background, rather than achievement.

2 Choose the correct alternative to complete the sentences.

1 When negotiating, _____.
   a) most cultures have the same approach
   b) Anglo-Americans do not need a team of negotiators
   c) personality differences are a key factor
   d) technical, psychological and cultural aspects need to be considered

2 In individualist countries, _____.
   a) people try to reach an agreement very quickly regardless of the cost
   b) negotiators do not have time to listen to their counterparts
   c) negotiators are often given the authority to decide on the spot
   d) high-ranking individuals are entrusted with negotiating powers

3 In communitarian cultures, _____.
   a) people rarely negotiate alone
   b) people do not want to reach an agreement quickly
   c) consensus is very detailed
   d) decisions are always referred back to head office

4 In communitarian cultures, negotiations take longer because _____.
   a) decision-making is based on consensus agreement
   b) more attention is paid to detail
   c) everybody in the company has to be consulted
   d) there is more concern about power

3 Complete the text below using the words in brackets. You may have to change their form. The extract is an adapted version of purchasing instructions taken from an armed forces manual.

Procurement by negotiation is the art of reaching a common (1) _____ (understand), through bargaining, on the essentials of a contract such as delivery (2) _____ (specify), prices and terms. Because of the (3) _____ (interrelate) of these factors with many others, it is a complex art and requires the exercise of (4) _____ (judge), tact and common sense. The effective negotiator is like an astute (5) _____ (shop) able to assess the possibilities of bargaining with the seller. Only if there is an (6) _____ (aware) of relative bargaining power can a negotiator know where to be firm or where he/she may be flexible and make allowances or (7) _____ (concede) in prices or terms.

Listening and writing

1 ☊ Listen to Pío Verges, a management consultant, who is giving his opinion on the art and science of negotiation. Choose the correct alternative to complete the sentences.

1 One of the basic rules to remember is that _____.
  a) you can negotiate anything
  b) negotiators are allowed to specialise
  c) negotiators should specialise in particular areas

2 According to the speaker, publishers _____.
  a) have misled the public about the art of negotiation
  b) have sold many books about negotiation trends
  c) negotiate and work together with the press

3 Developing negotiating skills in one field means _____.
  a) you can negotiate in any field
  b) you may feel uncomfortable negotiating in another field
  c) you are not allowed to negotiate in another field

4 When negotiating, an effort should be made to _____.
  a) say "no"
  b) be positive
  c) create a good rapport

5 You also have to _____.
  a) be greedy
  b) understand the position and aims of your counterpart
  c) know how much your counterpart earns

6 In cross-cultural negotiations it's a good idea to have an advisor to _____.
  a) back you up
  b) act as an interpreter of both language and culture
  c) understand your culture

2 ☊ On page 43 are descriptions of four courses or seminars designed to help impro negotiation skills. You will hear three people discussing courses they have just been on or are about to go on. For each person (1–3) mark one letter (A, B, C, or D) for the course referred to.

1 ____   2 ____   3 ____

3 You work in the human resources department of a travel company. Your company is becoming more and more global and now does business in three continents. Why would the courses in Exercise 2 be valuable to your company?

Write a letter or e-mail asking for information about one of the courses advertised.

• Say who you represent.
• Say why you are interested in the course.
• Ask the course organisers to forward information either in the post or by e-mail about:
  – the course content
  – the qualifications and experience of the speakers/teaching staff
  – the dates and prices
  – the number of participants per course/seminar
• Explain that your organisation/company wants to see references from people that have been on the course previously.
• Explain that you need to receive the information quite quickly (you have to present a staff training budget for your department before the end of the quarter).

A

NEGOTIATING ACROSS CULTURES

Are you prepared to go into full-scale negotiations with a foreign counterpart? What barriers are you likely to face? Is your approach to negotiation individualist or communitarian? And what is your counterpart's approach likely to be? This weekend seminar will take you all over the world as we examine challenges created by different languages, cultures, body language and company cultures. Being aware of these differences can save time, money and headaches.

For more information call **666 777 888**. Global Training Inc. 3127 Paseo de Roxas, 0722 Makati City, Philippines goglobal@phol.com

C

NEGOTIATING BY TELEPHONE AND E-MAIL

Enhance your communication.

- *Learn how to organise negotiations more efficiently by using the phone and e-mail more effectively.*
- *Learn how to improve your written and spoken expression to state and query aspects of the negotiation more effectively.*
- *Practise negotiating over the phone and hear yourself speak.*

One-day initiation seminar; four-day course.

Tel 300 333 300 or e-mail commtraining@ intl.com

B

ASSERTIVE NEGOTIATION
DISCOVER HOW TO NEGOTIATE ASSERTIVELY, NOT AGGRESSIVELY.
Learn to listen actively; to use body language appropriately; to use language effectively.
Learn to define your counterpart: assertive, non-assertive, aggressive, keen on rules, a bargainer...

One-day seminar with optional follow-up sessions. Book now. Call **907 607 607 607** for more information. UBU, 65 Granger Av., Northland 63090. ubu@ ubu.info

D

MULTIMEDIA COURSE IN CROSS-CULTURAL NEGOTIATION

The International Centre for Cross-cultural Training proudly presents its multimedia course in cross-cultural negotiation. A series of seminars to choose from, depending on where your company does business. In-depth analysis of your company's needs, thorough preparation of staff for effective negotiating. Tailor-made in-house seminars available on request.

*E-mail us for information at **iccct@wwn.coop***

C Speaking

Bargaining

Bargaining is often a matter of give and take: accepting or rejecting proposals, making counter-proposals or offering extras all form part of the process.
Match the sentences 1–9 with the functions a–i.

1 If we lowered the price, we'd be unable to provide the same quality and we're certainly not willing to give second-rate service.
2 No, I'm afraid we simply can't do that.
3 That sounds just fine.
4 We could probably consider lowering the price, if you decided to offer us the running of your in-company catering.
5 I'll definitely look into that and get back to you.
6 Well, we can arrange the catering for special occasions, but only if we have a couple of days' notice.
7 What sort of extras were you thinking of?
8 What about including coffee or tea?
9 Would you like us to put some flowers on the table?

a) accepting with a condition
b) accepting without any conditions
c) drawing the other party out
d) linking an offer to a counter-proposal
e) making a suggestion
f) offering to study the proposal
g) offering an extra service
h) rejecting a suggestion
i) rejecting a suggestion and explaining why

1 What are your attitudes to negotiating? First answer the questions on your own, preparing reasons for your choice. Then compare your views.

1 What's the best time of the morning to negotiate?
  a) first thing in the morning
  b) mid-morning
  c) just before lunch

2 Which negotiation situation do you feel most comfortable in?
  a) one-to-one
  b) group-to-group
  c) one-to-group

3 When you are negotiating, you should …
  a) speak more slowly than usual
  b) speak more loudly than usual
  c) neither of the above

4 In a negotiation, should you ….
  a) exaggerate what you want in order to achieve your real aims?
  b) state very clearly what you want and settle for no less than that?
  c) be prepared to compromise halfway?

5 Which of the following do you agree with?
  a) negotiating is more difficult than re-negotiating
  b) re-negotiating is more difficult than negotiating
  c) negotiating and re-negotiating are equally difficult

6 You're in the middle of a negotiation.
   The other party suddenly comes up
   with an unexpected alternative.
   What do you do?
   a) give a decision on the spot
   b) ask for time to consider the
       alternative
   c) excuse yourself and consult your
       line manager immediately

2 This role play is for two speakers.

Sauberlink manufactures cleaning
products. It supplies clients from all
over the world. At least twice a week,
clients are taken out for lunch. The
restaurant Sauberlink staff normally go
to has changed hands and no longer provides a satisfactory service. A team has
been to the other restaurants in the area. Chez Pierre is somewhat more
expensive than the others, but the quality of the food is excellent. The
management of Sauberlink has decided to approach Chez Pierre to discuss the
matter.

A works for Sauberlink and is in charge of public relations.
B is the owner of Chez Pierre.

A looks at this page. B turns to page 78.

SPEAKER A

Chez Pierre is your best option and you know they can provide the standard of
food that a company of your size and reputation needs. You want the restaurant
to provide the following:
- a private dining room
- a first-class menu
- a choice of dishes
- a range of dishes suitable for customers from the Middle and Far East
- a global price per person (18–22 euros pp including beverages, certainly not
  above 25 euros unless previously agreed to). Payment at the end of the
  month.

Scheduling:
Sometimes it is difficult to stipulate the exact time of the lunch – you want
approximately 30 minutes' flexibility on this. You can normally give a week's
notice for a booking but occasionally this is not possible. Meetings may be
cancelled at the last minute. (What are you prepared to offer in such cases?)

Other services:
The restaurant you used to go to was unable to do in-house entertaining
(cocktails for product launches in the showroom and so on), which an outside
caterer is doing an excellent job of. Would Chez Pierre be able to do it as well,
and if so, at what price?

3 All representatives of Sauberlink form one group. All members of Chez Pierre
   form another group.

Compare and contrast how your negotiation went, what the outcome was and
what further steps you think should be taken.

Where's the market?

KEY VOCABULARY

1 Combine words from the box to form phrases commonly used in marketing, eg *market + share = market share*.
You may use the same word twice.

> brand   commission   launch   loyal   market   sales   product
> researcher   share   study   target   niche

2 Use the phrases to complete the definitions below.

1 A person who always buys the same product is _____.

2 A group of consumers and potential consumers is a company's

   _____.

3 A _____ is a relatively small or specialised part of a larger market for goods or services.

4 A person who investigates the needs and reactions of (potential) consumers is a _____. He/she carries out a _____.

5 When a product is shown to the public for the first time, we talk about a

   _____.

6 Of the total number of goods sold, the percentage one manufacturer sells is

   its _____.

7 A sales representative or agent may be paid a percentage of the value of products or services sold. This is called a _____.

A Listening

1 🎧 Listen to Leonard Exter Spector, Executive Vice-President of Audits and Surveys Inc, a market research company in the US, answer the question: Why do firms consult market research companies?

Complete the summary below using up to three words for each gap.

> Products sometimes fail because the company that launches the product has misjudged the potential reaction of the marketplace to this new product. A number of reasons and examples were given for why market research is _carried out_____.
>
> The coffee industry wanted to know why coffee sales
> (1) _____. They found out that people were
> drinking more (2) _____ and less coffee as a result
> of (3) _____. The method used to find out this
> information was (4) _____.

Advertising a product (5) _____ is very expensive. Message recall (whether people remember what a commercial is saying) is important, so before running a TV commercial, a company might ask a market researcher to test alternative versions to determine (6) _____ are being remembered.

A car manufacturer tested initial reactions to its latest model by inviting a small panel of (7) _____ to test out the car. The initial reaction (8) _____. People thought that the car was considerably (9) _____ than it really was. On closer examination, market researchers discovered that (10) _____ was responsible for creating this impression.

These examples demonstrate that an individual cannot presume to know the opinion of the general public, or guess the public's responses to a given product.

2　You are going to hear part of a radio programme. Wayne Newton, a businessman, is being interviewed about how he developed a niche market.

Choose the correct alternative to complete the sentences.

1　Wayne set up a business because _____.
   a)　he liked being outside
   b)　his own interests led him to identify a gap in the market
   c)　he had always wanted to set up a mail-order business

2　The company went on-line because _____.
   a)　they saw the possibilities and approached another company to form part of their site
   b)　they thought it would be a worthwhile feature
   c)　another company suggested that they form part of their site

3　The alliance with BASOL did not _____.
   a)　guarantee long-term success
   b)　have a very positive effect on sales figures
   c)　allow them to give a better service

4　Market share was eroded by booksdirect, probably because _____.
   a)　booksdirect was getting 900,000 hits a day
   b)　booksdirect's prices were better
   c)　booksdirect's catalogue was cheaper

5　The solution was _____.
   a)　to change the alliance with BASOL
   b)　to diversify
   c)　to change the focus of the company and sell adventure journeys

6　booksdirect did not sell products like rare books _____.
   a)　because there was no market for them
   b)　because they did not like that type of product
   c)　but no clear reason is given as to why this is so

7　The company employs outdoor adventurers because _____.
   a)　they can help and advise customers based on their own experience
   b)　they will identify better with their jobs
   c)　they can teach people hang-gliding and bungee-jumping

8　Wayne opened a shop _____.
   a)　to expand the business
   b)　to attract new customers
   c)　for public relations and marketing

KEY VOCABULARY

Describing trends

Look at the table. Identify at least one word or expression in each column that does not describe the trend indicated.

↗ upward movement		↘ downward movement		↔ little or no change	
climb	rise	come down	plummet	bounce back	remain constant
drop	rocket	decrease	plunge	even out	remain stable
go up	soar	fall	sink	hold	slide
improve	take off	go down	slip	level off	stabilise
pick up		hold steady		peak	

1 When the Sambaramba Centre opened in April it was an instant success. However, the success story did not last long. Look at the newspaper stories and the graph, which details average weekend turnover during that time. Then complete the sentences below using words from the *Key vocabulary* above.

Personalities from the worlds of fashion, film and theatre filled the Sambaramba Centre when it opened on 1st April in Breaker Bay. The complex has three dance floors, four bars and other facilities. It is equipped with the latest technology in sound and lighting, has ample parking (400 cars) and shuttle transport to take clientele to and from the city centre.

August 15th Jade opened its doors this week to the sound of the Scooders. Fans flocked to this new venue; many were unable to get in. The club, in the heart of the city, aims to attract locals and tourists alike. It has two superb dance floors, quiet lounge areas and a snack bar. It plans to host live groups at weekends.

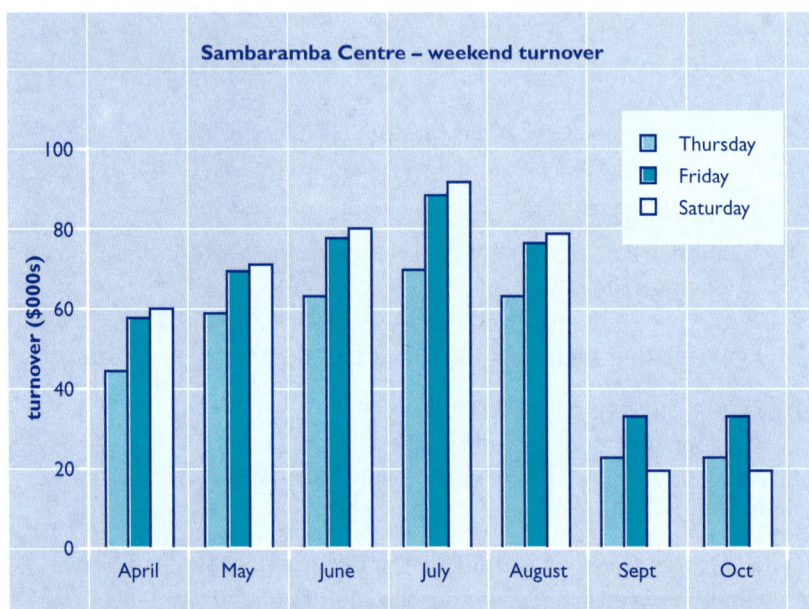

Sambaramba Centre – weekend turnover

1 For the first three months weekend turnover ...
2 In July, turnover ...
3 When Jade opened, turnover ...
4 In September, weekend turnover ...
5 In October, turnover ...

2 What can the Sambaramba do to bring back clientele? Work with a partner. Look at the suggestions below. Add at least two more alternatives for each category. Then talk about the options, giving reasons why they might or might not be effective in the case of the Sambaramba.

Market research
a) analyse the type of clientele going to Jade
b) carry out a survey of other popular night venues for benchmarking purposes

Marketing strategies
a) define target clientele and cater for them only
b) create a loyal clientele (have a membership card offering special rates and discounts for services)

Special promotions
a) put on live shows
b) reduce mid-week entry fee

3 This activity requires at least two pairs of students. Each pair will receive information on an adverse marketing situation.

After you have discussed the information and alternatives in your pairs, one student in the first pair will give a report to the others describing the current situation. The other student in the first pair will then present a marketing strategy describing the steps you propose to take to restore the image of the company or product.

After the presentations, other students may ask questions. Then the students in the second pair take turns to give their presentations.

The first pair looks at the information on this page. The second pair looks at the information on page 79.

PAIR A

Lecker Ice-creams' sales have slumped following reports that whale fat has been used to make the ice-cream creamier.

Key events:

July: Reports and rumours start circulating about the quality of the ice-cream.

July: Lecker management is asked about the matter and denies the accusation.

August: A consumer organisation publishes an analysis of ice-cream. Lecker appears in the group of manufacturers with doubtful ingredients (eg whale fat).

September: Save the Whale campaign launched worldwide. Consumers asked to boycott any products containing whale derivatives.

November: Lecker removes all ice-cream from stores and launches a new product.

December: Sales continue to be below expectations.

Possible strategies:

- Employ a market research company to discover reasons why the new product has not been successful and come up with possible solutions. *(may be expensive and time-consuming)*
- Target restaurant/catering sectors, especially entertainment parks. *(lower profit margin, but new market)*
- Re-launch using a new brand name.
- Create a new brand image. *(time-consuming)*
- Test new flavours.
- Initiate publicity campaign highlighting changed ingredients.
- Promote the ice-cream through discreet product placement in sitcom or soap opera TV shows.
- Give promotional items with ice-creams, eg stickers, vouchers for free ice-creams, etc.

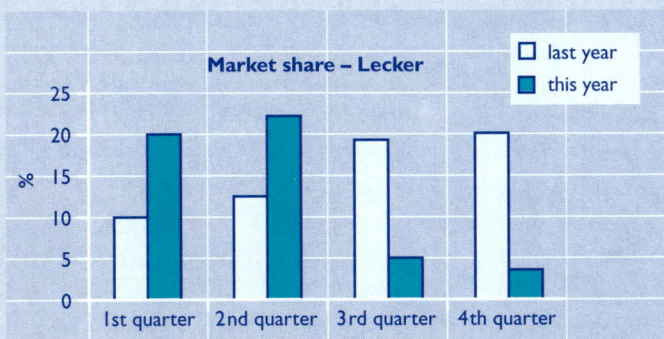

Market share – Lecker

□ last year
■ this year

(Bar chart showing % market share by quarter. Vertical axis labelled % from 0 to 25. 1st quarter: last year 10, this year 20. 2nd quarter: last year 12, this year 22. 3rd quarter: last year 20, this year 5. 4th quarter: last year 21, this year 4.)

Reading and writing

"What made radio and television a good business is that they were limited to three networks." (Ted Turner, founder of CNN, to TV executives' annual convention, 1999)

1 Read the magazine editorial below about the changing nature of the economics of the television industry. Choose the correct alternative to fill each gap.

The proliferation of television channels has led to the fragmentation of the (1) _____. In fact, it was Ted Turner himself who changed the (2) _____ of history by creating his cable empire. The (3) _____ underlying Turner's comments is as follows: in the first place, with a growing number of channels, advertisers are less and less convinced about the (4) _____ of using this medium (and advertising is a primary source of income for television broadcasters). Secondly, technological progress means that the number of channels (5) _____ will become even greater in the not-too-distant future.

Where does this leave the economics of the broadcasters? How will it affect the advertising industry in general? Will advertising expenditure be able to (6) _____ sufficiently to be shared by all? How will audience ratings be monitored? Will television advertising disappear altogether, with viewers paying as they view?

Such were the questions (7) _____

this sector of the economy at the start of the new millennium. Companies went to great lengths to attract audiences, push up the ratings and (8) _____ in advertising revenues. Human tragedy and emotion depicted in war, earthquakes, shootouts and so on seemed to be the only guarantee of an audience. Plans to blow up a large passenger plane on purpose, contests to marry a millionaire and other schemes were (9) _____ in an effort to attract audiences. Marketing experts examined new avenues, particularly on the internet, to (10) _____ their target consumer or user. In the United States, the television companies (11) _____ alliances or merged with apparent rivals, both within the industry itself and with internet companies, to abate the negative effects intensified competition and technology were having on their advertising revenues and (12) _____ on their profits. These developments have had several implications for the industry worldwide and will continue to influence it.

1 a) audience	b) audiences	c) public	d) spectators
2 a) run	b) picture	c) course	d) book
3 a) rationale	b) reason	c) basis	d) fear
4 a) profit	b) yield	c) return	d) viability
5 a) shown	b) available	c) are there	d) around
6 a) advance	b) grow	c) rise	d) grow up
7 a) addressing	b) posing to	c) asking	d) facing
8 a) draw	b) attract	c) guide	d) channel
9 a) imagined	b) achieved	c) devised	d) drawn
10 a) reach	b) achieve	c) arrive to	d) touch
11 a) did	b) took over	c) formed	d) realised
12 a) too	b) as well	c) so	d) therefore

2 Read the text below. It is about people in their late teens and early twenties, sometimes known as Generation Y. In most of the numbered lines there is one extra word. It is either grammatically incorrect or illogical. Identify the extra words and cross them out. Then discuss the text together.

Where's the market gone?

1 Spotting consumer trends is big business. Up until ~~too~~ recently, the job of

2 researchers and analysts, sometimes known as marketeers, has been to gather

3 feedback on the concerns of consumers. In the 1990s, we, the consumers, invariably

4 have had to adapt to the product and that product was available wherever we

5 went. Those were the days of household names and brand loyalty. In the so hi-

6 tech culture we are moving into, the product is having to adapt to the consumer.

7 With exposure to multimedia has created a shift in values, attitudes and behaviour.

8 Today's youth, for example, the so-called Y generation, are consumers of the high-

9 speed information. Their reactions to advertisements are different from those of

10 previous generations. The internet encourages diversity and this generation has

11 become, the high analysts are saying, a labyrinth of niche markets. Brand loyalty

12 doesn't exist for them. Hot names change quickly: what's not fashionable one

13 month may no longer be so the next. Previous generations formed a relatively

14 homogenous market. This one which has forced a shift from mass-produced to more

15 personalised or personalised-looking products. Hence the less industrial look of

16 the latest hi-tech products. Tapping these markets may be well be the road

17 to success. Certainly, companies that do not move with and respond to these

18 changes are going to miss them out.

3 You have been asked by a manufacturer to do some market research to ensure that a new hi-tech product (eg a digital video game) will appeal to the target market, namely Generation Y.

1 Work in pairs or threes. Discuss how you will get in touch with your market (internet? magazines? school and other education centres? youth clubs? sports clubs?). Discuss how you will conduct the research (small panel, focus group or questionnaire? in-depth interviews or random spot interviews?).

2 Use the following outline to write a preliminary proposal stating how you intend to carry out your research.

Introduction
State the purpose of the research. Give background information if you wish.

Main part
Outline one or more options. For each option state the following information:

• how contact with the target market will be established
• how the research will be carried out
• estimated duration of the investigation

Summary
Mention possibilities to extend services offered (eg representative groups can be created for detailed market testing) or follow up in the future.

Right place, right time

KEY VOCABULARY

Complete the following definitions using the words or phrases below.

1   A company or country has **competitive advantage** when it can

_____ products or services _____ than its

competitors.

2   **Fleet management** refers to the scheduling, co-ordination and control of a
number of vehicles being used to _____ from one place to
another.

3   The term **idle stocks** refers to goods that are not being used for any purpose,

and are therefore not _____ any _____.

4   In order to be able to send information _____ to another the
software must be **integrated**.

5   **Logistics systems** are computer-based programmes used to manage and

co-ordinate _____ which is moving from one place to another.

6   **Satellite tracking** is an intelligent transport system whereby the

_____ is monitored via satellite.

7   **Supply chain management** is the co-ordination and control of the inward and

outward _____ that form part of the production process –
from the inward delivery of raw materials to the outward delivery of the
finished product.

a) delivery of all products	f) transport goods
b) from one computer	g) merchandise
c) generating	h) supply
d) position of merchandise	i) on more favourable terms
e) revenue	

A   Reading

1   Read the text on page 53 and then choose the best heading for each paragraph in
the text from a–g below.

1 ____
2 ____
3 ____
4 ____
5 ____

a) A Matter of Research
b) Adapting to the Times: Will They Cope?
c) What Really Counts
d) Software Solutions
e) The Effect of Global Production
f) Integrating Software
g) Who'll Manage the Chain?

1 Why is one supplier chosen over another? Is it a matter of price? service? reliability? In the middle of 1999 a well-known firm of consultants published research which showed that cost was no longer the most important factor when it came to choosing a supplier. According to the research, the key to winning orders lies in the ability to provide a good service. Above all, products have to be delivered to the right place, at the right time and in the right condition.

2 The more manufacturers and retailers operate on a global basis, the more important logistics become. This is because distribution networks have become more complex and require tighter management. When a company is importing supplies from a number of sources, assembling products and then distributing them to a larger number of venues, managing every step in the supply chain is imperative. Co-ordination and scheduling are essential. If one piece of a machine arrives late the whole production run will be delayed or even suspended. This may mean stocks and employees lying idle. Any accumulation of unnecessary stocks means tying up resources such as space and money unproductively.

3 Many manufacturers and retailers, particularly the larger ones, have turned to supply chain management as a way of reducing costs and have applied the principles of minimal stocks and shifting stocks from one store to another as a cost-cutting measure. One of the major problems many companies face is that their software packages for logistics systems are not integrated and are sometimes not even compatible. In other words, they may have a good programme for managing stocks, another programme for transportation (trucking and fleet management), and another one again for orders. Firms that buy out a competitor or a supplier often find that the software used by the newly acquired division is incompatible with that of the parent company. This can lead to the business running a wide range of unrelated computer systems, which does not help to make the logistics management of the supply chain efficient and effective. In addition, when a wide range of unintegrated software is being used along the chain, information is not easily shared. For this very reason, most if not all major retailers insist that their suppliers use the software packages they stipulate. In this way, as soon as a product is bought in a retail outlet, this information is recorded and sent by the cash register directly to the supplier, who then knows how many products need to be replaced.

4 A company can either manage the supply chain itself or subcontract or outsource the managing of the chain to another company. Finding a third party that will manage the chain for you is not as easy as it sounds. Logistics consultants abound, but they give advice and set up systems rather than actually manage them. On the whole, freight forwarders have not moved as quickly as they might to corner this potential market. There are, however, a few exceptions to be found, particularly among former courier companies, many of whom use satellite tracking and other intelligent transport systems.

5 In Europe, it has been the post offices, whose future seemed unsure to many at the beginning of the 1990s, who have got on the logistics bandwagon, spurred on, some say, by the advent of the single market and monetary system, together with the growth of the e-commerce sector. They face the challenge inherent in changing from being a monopoly that provided a mail service to becoming a professionally competent logistics operator in a fiercely competitive market. This implies fundamental changes in terms of mentality and organisation. Their management will have to be trained sufficiently if they are to succeed in establishing a new role in tomorrow's world of business.

2 Choose the correct alternative to complete the sentences.

1 Price is _____ when people choose a product or a service.
   a) the overriding factor
   b) not taken into account
   c) one of several factors

2 The importance of logistics is growing _____.
   a) with the globalisation of the marketplace
   b) because globalisation increases idle stocks
   c) to avoid stock accumulation

3 With software, it's often the case that _____.
   a) different departments use different software
   b) companies are unequipped to manage the supply chain
   c) newly acquired companies use the same system

4 Experts are surprised that the freight industry _____.
   a) was eager to expand into logistics
   b) did not have software to manage supply chains
   c) let potential business go elsewhere

5 The major challenge for the post offices _____.
   a) lies in how to cope with the growth of e-commerce
   b) is how to change from a monopoly mentality to a competitive one
   c) is how to overcome their lack of professional competence

Listening and writing

1 🎧 Nelson Computers is a hardware supplier. They pride themselves on being able to meet orders within a minimum time. They work with the latest technology to control the movement of stocks. Lassaters is a hotel chain which has recently bought out a group of hotels and is standardising and upgrading its information systems. Lassaters have chosen Nelson Computers to supply essential hardware.

You will hear five brief telephone conversations relating to the fulfilment of the order Lassaters places with Nelson Computers. The following employees are involved or mentioned by name.

- Simon Gale, Sales Department, Nelson Computers
- Veronica Smythe, Purchasing Department, Lassaters
- Peter MacFarnan, Logistics Department, Nelson Computers
- Toni Fiorello, Inventory Services Manager, Nelson Computers
- Susan Cleaver, Customer Services Director, Nelson Computers

Match each conversation with one of the descriptions a–g below.

1 ____   3 ____   5 ____

2 ____   4 ____

The purpose of the call is to:

a) complain about an overdue order
b) correct an order that has been placed
c) discuss a supply problem
d) enquire about an overdue order
e) explain the details of an overdue order
f) inform a customer about the delivery of an order
g) place an order

2 Summarise the events in chronological order.

First of all, Lassaters ordered 500 computers from Nelson Computers who, by mistake ...
Then ...
After that ...
A few days later ...
Finally ...

3 Susan Cleaver, Customer Services Director for Nelson Computers, receives regular written updates on any problems with important orders. On 19th April Peter MacFarnan wrote to inform Susan Cleaver of the situation regarding the Lassaters order.

Complete his e-mail using one appropriate word for each gap.

Nelson Computers 3.37 pm

✎ **E-MAIL FOR SUSAN CLEAVER**

To: Susan Cleaver
Date: April 19th
From: Peter MacFarnan
Subject: Lassaters order (500 N745s)

We (1) _____ just received an e-mail from the factory saying they are (2) _____

to assemble the N745s because some parts (3) _____ not arrived. I decided to call Transglo

as (4) _____ are co-ordinating this order.

The goods have been held (5) _____ because of monsoon rains. The weather might

(6) _____ within the next two days, but this is uncertain.

This (7) _____ is now going to be overdue and Lassaters (8) _____ start complaining

soon. I suggest that we (9) _____ them of the situation and then look for alternative solutions

(10) _____ as re-routing or using a different source.

WRITING TIPS

A letter of complaint

An effective letter of complaint:
- starts off in a direct but polite manner
- mentions the complaint in the opening paragraph
- describes the problem clearly
- draws the company's attention to what needs to be corrected
- requests or suggests a solution

---

4 In the fourth extract, Veronica Smythe phones Nelson Computers for the second time to complain about the delay in the order.

1 Immediately after calling Nelson Computers on 22nd April, Veronica Smythe decides to write to Susan Cleaver, Customer Services Director, to complain not only about the delay (and the problems this is causing Lassaters), but also about the unhelpful attitude of the Sales Department staff. Use the guidelines above to write Veronica Smythe's letter.

2 Exchange letters with your partner. It is 9 am on 24th April. Nelson's staff have been working on the problem and have found a solution. To give an impression of efficiency, and for the purpose of good public relations, you (Susan Cleaver) decide to fax or e-mail a reply to Veronica Smythe's letter, which is to be followed up by a call (the last conversation on the tape) arranging delivery.

Before writing the letter, discuss the following:

- What is the purpose of the letter?
- How should you begin?
- Which of the following will you do?

  – thank Ms Smythe for her letter
  – apologise for the situation and any inconvenience caused
  – explain the cause of the problem
  – explain what has been or will be done to solve the problem
  – reply to any requests made in Ms Smythe's letter
  – point out that your service is normally good
  – assure Ms Smythe that Lassaters is a valued customer
  – encourage Ms Smythe to get in touch again if necessary

C Speaking

KEY LANGUAGE

Making enquiries and complaints

1 Read the following sentences and match them with their functions (a–f) below.

1 Is there any possibility of using a faster delivery route? _____

2 Could you please tell us by midday what the current situation is? _____

3 I'm very sorry about the delay; we're doing all we can to make up for lost time. _____

4 Listen, we expected these goods to arrive yesterday, you know. _____

5 Look, this is really putting us in a very difficult situation. _____

6 The current situation in the area is making it difficult to get supplies through. _____

7 We may have to look elsewhere for these products, you know. _____

8 We sent you an e-mail but haven't received a reply. _____

9 We'd like to know what the situation is regarding our Order q227.

10 What about using a different supplier? _____

a) apologise for a situation
b) complain about a situation
c) explain the reason for a delay
d) request information
e) suggest alternatives
f) threaten to make other arrangements

2 This role play is for two speakers.

A works for Sanicui, a wholesaler and distributor of drugs to chemists and supermarkets. B works for Appolinus, a large drugs manufacturer.

Recently a serious epidemic of flu has been affecting all sections of the community. Hospitals are full, medical stocks are low and the newspapers are full of health scare stories. Appolinus manufactures a very effective flu treatment and there is now considerable demand for it. Sanicui is under pressure from chemists and supermarkets to supply more of it. Treatments from other manufacturers are available but Appolinus's product is the most popular.

A looks at page 57. B turns to page 80.

SPEAKER A

Sanicui

Background information:

- You have been dealing with Appolinus for many years. Their record as a supplier is first-class.
- The current flu epidemic hit other countries before your own. You exported available stocks (this is very lucrative – 35–45% additional profit).
- You ordered supplies as soon as stocks started getting low. They should have arrived but haven't and now you only have supplies for 3.5 days (legal minimum 2.5 days).
- You need supplies urgently and they ought to be available at the normal price.

Options:

Source	Lead time	Cost difference	Observations
Appolinus	3–4 weeks	current supplier	Can they obtain supplies from an alternative source?
Salutus	2–4 days	+20%	Large minimum orders (amount = half present Appolinus order). Can you cancel part of the Appolinus order?
Rival laboratories in other countries	2–4 days	+35–50%	No business relationship established (and they may know about your "exports")

According to your information, Appolinus has the following options:

Source	Lead time	Cost difference	Observations
Peru	3–4 weeks	current supplier	Cancellation fee = ?
Brazil	3 days	+15–18%	Minimum order = ?
Colombia	2 days or 4 days	+25% or +15%	
Other	Synthetic substitutes available +32% cost, minimum 3 days' lead time		

When you are ready, call Appolinus. You want/need:

- an explanation as to why you have received no information on your order
- an update on supplies
- an immediate, short-term solution
- to minimise any extra costs you may have to pay (preferably none)

3 When you have reached a decision, write an e-mail to each other confirming the outcome of your discussion.

Staying ahead

discussing competitiveness

making and clarifying points

analysing opinions and situations

KEY CONCEPTS

Staying ahead of the competition is a major priority for many businesses today. They need to know what their competitors are doing, what their customers want and what their employees are capable of producing. Efficient management of information is essential. Using, sharing and updating the collective knowledge and expertise of employees is essential.

The following words and phrases are used when talking about being and staying ahead.

1 **Information management**: using information systems (eg data mining) for the sorting, updating, channelling, sharing, and use of information currently or potentially available to a company or organisation.

2 **Knowledge management**: a strategy that turns managed information plus the skills, talents and expertise of its employees into greater productivity, new value and greater competitiveness.

3 **Company mind-set**: the mentality and methodology of a company and its employees. It refers to ingrained ways of doing things, attitudes, working and managerial style.

4 **Re-engineering**: changing the organisational structure, systems and/or processes within a company; redesigning, streamlining business processes.

5 **Employee benefits**: extra items given to employees over and above salary, eg company car, lunch vouchers, grants for further education. Also known as **fringe benefits** or **perks**.

6 **Staff turnover**: the frequency with which employees leave and join an organisation.

A Reading

1 Look at the eight sentences below. They refer to the case studies on the opposite page in which knowledge management (KM) initiatives are described.

Which case does each sentence refer to? For each sentence, mark one letter (A–E).

1 The aim of this initiative was to save unnecessary work (and processing of information). ____

2 The main aim of this project was to regain market share. ____

3 The main purpose of this initiative was to improve customer service. ____

4 The underlying principle in this case is: employees are a valuable asset, keep them. ____

5 There was resistance to the new methods initially. ____

6 This case describes how to make more of the existing resources and know-how in a company. ____

7 This company had lost touch with its market and was organised inefficiently. ____

8 This company has modified its business activities as a result of KM. ____

A A Finnish metals smelting firm decided to use its accumulated expertise and set up a consulting division which not only advises on the construction of plants but also trains personnel and managers all over the world. This diversification has proved to be more profitable than the original smelting business itself.

B In the Swift Hotel Group, staff have cards on which they take notes of any and every personal encounter with a guest. This information, together with data obtained directly from the guests (for example when they request extra towels, how they like their boiled egg and so on), is stored in a database. Whenever a client returns to the hotel, his or her personal requirements are printed out and made known to all staff so that each guest receives highly personalised treatment.

C The SAS Institute, a software company based in North Carolina, has adopted the policy of keeping motivation high and staff turnover low as a means of producing quality software and consistent profits. The company offers better than average employee benefits, profit-sharing bonuses and a working culture that revolves around accountability, responsibility and trust. Why leave a company that values its employees and sees staff turnover as money lost rather than inevitable? Why leave a company where long working hours are frowned upon? Few have a good reason to do so. Staff turnover at SAS is under 5 per cent whereas the average for the sector is 20 per cent.

D When the Boeing 777 was built, instead of the traditional design team managing the construction, more than 200 teams were on the job, designing and constructing sub parts. All suppliers used the same database system, thus facilitating the flow of information. This improved workflow, because each party received only the information they needed (rather than all information regardless of whether it was really of interest to the team or not). Initially some teams suffered from "culture shock" and complained about not knowing absolutely everything. It took time to change their mind-set and make them understand that knowing everything only meant duplication of effort.

E An Asian property group appeared to be feeling the adverse effects of an increasingly competitive market much more than its competitors. A consulting group found that the company made assumptions about customers, the competition and the market conditions rather than basing their decisions on facts. In addition, their bureaucratic and hierarchical structure was inefficient and outmoded. Starting from the top, the consultants re-engineered the company, its processes and systems and changed the company mind-set. As a result, the retrained staff felt more committed to their work, staff morale rose and their services improved. With a competent, committed workforce, faster systems and a more efficient structure, the company regained the confidence of the marketplace.

2 Choose the best heading for each case study from 1–6 below. One of the headings is not used.

1 At Your Service ____

2 Flying Start ____

3 Getting Behind and Bouncing Back ____

4 Going into Action ____

5 Using Company Wisdom ____

6 Caring Is Profitable ____

3 Can you think of any examples where the following actions have helped a company to recover or to improve its performance?

- encouraging staff creativity
- improving staff conditions
- investing more in market research
- re-structuring the organisation

B Listening

1 🎧 The company you work for has sent you to a seminar on knowledge management.

You will hear Sandra Jefferson-Coombs opening the seminar. Listen to her welcoming speech and mark the sentences below true or false.

1	Ms Jefferson-Coombs studied with Dr Dickler.	T	F
2	Dr Dickler said that in the future, power would depend on having access to information.	T	F
3	It is going to be relatively easy to bring the internet to developing nations.	T	F
4	The internet has changed what we can do with information.	T	F
5	In spite of the development of information technologies, work is much the same as in the past.	T	F
6	Businesses and organisations need to find the best ways of using the information they have access to.	T	F
7	There will be some important speakers at the seminar.	T	F

2 🎧 The seminar organisers, IKM Consultants, have sent you this programme of events.

You will hear Michael Albright talking about the programme, and outlining changes to it and additional information. Complete the information on page 61.

IKM Consultants

Pan-Pacific Knowledge Management Congress

10–11 May Toona Convention Centre

PROGRAMME OF EVENTS

10 May

8.00	Registration
8.30–9.30	Official welcome Inaugural speech by Dr David Gordon, University of Dallas Graduate School of Management: *The Role of the Global Manager in an Information Society*

Information Management

9.30–10.30	*The Answer Centre – an Information Catalyst*
	COFFEE BREAK
11.00–12.00	*From the Designer's Table to the Store in Two Weeks: An Example of Efficient Information Management* (customer information, logistics and stock control)
12.00–12.45	Round-table discussion with on-line links: *Administration and Information Management – At the Citizens' Service*
	LUNCH BREAK

Skills and Capability Management

14.00–15.00	a) *Using Training to Build Loyalty and Raise Productivity and Profits* b) *Keeping Staff Up-to-date*
15.00–16.00	*Making the Most out of Know-how*
	COFFEE BREAK
16.30–17.30	Round-table discussion: *The Principles Underlying KM*
20.00	Conference dinner-dance: venue to be confirmed

Collaboration and Knowledge-sharing

8.30–9.30	*Shareware – What Does It Really Mean?*
9.30–10.30	*Know-how Sharing Using a New Knowledge-sharing System – the Japanese Experience*
	C O F F E E B R E A K
11.00–12.00	*Office Design and Knowledge-sharing*
12.00–12.45	*Intranets, Knowledge-sharing and Team-building – The Role of Consultants*
	L U N C H B R E A K

General

14.00–15.00	*Changing Mind-sets – What Does It Involve?*
15.00–16.00	*Shareholder Value – How KM Generates Value*
	C O F F E E B R E A K
16.30–17.30	Closing session: *Measuring Knowledge as an Asset – Four Views*

Part 1

Initially Mr Albright makes a few general comments. As you listen, complete the sentences below using up to three words for each gap.

1 All changes can be checked _____ or on bulletin boards.

2 _____ will be held in either the Charman Room or the Mansfield Room.

3 Video and on-line conferences will be held _____.

4 All sessions begin _____ the scheduled hour.

5 If you arrive late you _____ to enter.

6 To access events on-line you _____ your password.

Part 2

Listen to the changes to the programme and additional information mentioned and complete the sentences and gaps 1–10 below.

Sessions
10 May
14.00 *Keeping Staff Up-to-date* has been (1) _____

Making the Most out of Know-how will be held in the (2) _____

16.30 Round-table discussion now on (3) _____
11 May
8.30–9.30 New talk: (4) "_____"

Additional information
(write down where to go for the following and any other relevant information)

Software companies: (5) _____

KM and staff training consultants: (6) _____

Information booths, cafés, lounges: (7) _____

To recharge mobile phones and laptops: (8) _____

Dinner-dance venue: (9) _____

Reservations: (10) _____

3 Discuss which three sessions at the seminar would interest you most and why.

Speaking and writing

KEY EXPRESSIONS

Match the two parts of the sentences below, which contain expressions for making your point in a discussion.

1 **As far as I'm concerned**, if we want to survive,

2 **As I see it**, one of our biggest problems

3 **I feel** very strongly that we are unable to do our job properly

4 **In my view**, the reason people have stopped shopping here is that

5 **It seems to me** that head office makes decisions without

A because we're not given enough information or in-service training.

B consulting those who have to carry out their new plan.

C is the quality and range of goods.

D staff change all the time.

E we'll have to offer our customers something extra.

1 A retail department store chain, Johnson and Lilley, is running into difficulties: its turnover is down and falling, customer complaints are frequent and rising and there is a lack of co-ordination and group spirit in its head office.

Look at the following opinions expressed by five members of staff. In each case the first sentence is missing. Choose from the sentences in the *Key expressions* above to complete what was said.

a) James Clarke, Sales Assistant

"_____ **What I'm saying is**, customers like being able to recognise 'their' shop assistant, it makes them loyal and feel secure; it's someone they can trust. If there's a new face every other day they feel anonymous and that's not always what they want."

b) Paula Hargreaves, Sales (women's fashion)

"_____ **It's quite clear that** the buyers are off track. I wouldn't be seen dead in some of the things we have on sale. Customers have started complaining about the quality too – quality used to be our hallmark."

c) Justin Browning, Sales

"_____ **What I mean is**, nobody ever asks us for our opinions, yet we know a lot about customer behaviour and preferences. We're like puppets: we're told to shift products from one end of the store to the other overnight, without really knowing why, and then customers can never find anything, get angry and leave."

d) Shona Armousch, Customer Relations

"_____ **As a result** we often can't answer customers' questions, you know, like when a particular product will be back in stock. We often can't give them advice either on how to use or care for products, and people don't like that, they want to have answers."

e) Sara Lawami, newly appointed Marketing Manager

"_____ **In other words**, added value that our competitors cannot match – that means good service, knowledge about our products, personalised treatment, on-line solutions and so on."

2 Imagine you are one of the people in Exercise 1. Using the expressions **in bold**, discuss:

- how the problems mentioned affect the company's ability to compete
- how the problems might be solved

3 This role play is for four speakers.

You all work for a firm of consultants. The company has asked you to explore ways of bringing the organisation back on track.
Each of you specialises in one area:

A: Market research – your information is on this page.
B: Human resources – turn to page 81.
C: Information technology – turn to page 81.
D: Management and team-building – turn to page 81.

You have carried out initial research to examine the reasons for the company's current situation. A meeting has been called to discuss your findings and to reach a decision on what recommendations to make.

Use the information on your cards and the words in bold in Exercise 1 above to express your views.

SPEAKER A

Market research

Main problems:

- company has lost touch with the market
- contradiction between target market expressed through advertising (16–25), product lines (25–40) and real clientele (35 +)

Solutions:

- carry out thorough market research to discover:
  - why customers have left
  - why certain customers remain loyal
  - what these target groups (ie current and former customers) want
- test pilot collections (on potential customers) to gauge market response
- create an improved customer database to steer future marketing efforts in the right direction

4 Based on the discussion you have just had, use the following guidelines to write the executive summary to a long report on behalf of the consultants.

1 Introduction: purpose of and background to the report	3 Analysis of findings (by area)
2 Summary of findings	4 Conclusions and recommendations to the Board of Directors

It's a free world

discussing international trade

reporting comments

describing conditions for foreign investment

KEY VOCABULARY

International trade

1 Complete the following definitions using a word or noun phrase from the box. You may need to modify the term slightly to make it grammatically correct.

arbitration	balance of payments	dumping	import duty
protectionism	quota	sanctions	surplus	tariff

1 The difference between imports (trade expenditure) and exports (trade revenue) is expressed as the _____.

2 If two countries disagree on the interpretation of trade agreements, an independent _____ is called in to settle the dispute.

3 If a country does not adhere to international trade agreements, _____ are frequently applied as a type of punishment.

4 Overproduction of goods and bumper harvests may result in a _____ unless demand increases sufficiently. This glut in the market will normally lead to a fall in prices.

5 If a country deliberately charges less in one market than in another and sells goods below the cost of production, we call this _____.

6 Restrictions on imports, either expressed in quantity limits (_____), or through restrictions of a bureaucratic nature, are often imposed to save local production. This is known as _____.

A Listening

MEXICO – EU Talk Trade

EU–US Trade War in Sight

Protection or Protectionism?
Tokyo under Fire from Washington

1 Listen to a radio reporter giving a summary of a speech by Mike Moore, Director General of the World Trade Organisation, to developing-country ministers in 1999.

Look at the nine statements below. Decide whether they are true or false and note key words or expressions to justify your view.

Mike Moore said that:
1 Developing nations needed more technical assistance.   T   F
2 The poorest nations should be charged duty on their exports.   T   F
3 Not all countries felt the same about free trade.   T   F
4 Predictions about the economic prospects of developing nations had been accurate.   T   F

5 A fall in prices for raw materials seriously affected the poorest nations. T   F
6 Political stability was vital for development.   T   F
7 Trade would benefit the least developed nations.   T   F
8 Tariffs are high in sectors such as textiles and agriculture.   T   F
9 Current international trade legislation needed to be changed.   T   F

Now read the tapescript on page 90 and write two new true/false statements for your partner to listen for. Exchange statements and listen to the recording again.

2 🎧 Armand Basi is the owner of a textile company in Spain. Listen to his opinion on how the textile industry in his country is affected by free trade and choose the correct alternative to complete the sentences.

1 Protectionism in the textile industry often exists in countries where

   _____.

   a) it is a traditional industry
   b) the industry is fundamental to the economy
   c) textiles are economical to produce

2 The textile market in Spain _____.

   a) has always been free
   b) has just become free
   c) has been free for some time

3 Globalisation is _____.

   a) inevitable
   b) democratic
   c) a short-term trend

4 Manufacturers have not moved factories from one country to another because

   _____.

   a) they haven't been able to
   b) it makes it impossible to get goods to market
   c) it does not always make economic sense

5 Which of the following make global production complex? _____.

   a) setting up the plant properly
   b) additional expenses for technical staff
   c) timing, co-ordination and distribution

6 In the future the textile industry in industrialised nations _____.

   a) will survive in spite of industrialisation
   b) will have to innovate and provide a good service in order to survive
   c) will not need labour

1 Before you read discuss the following questions:
  • Where are bananas grown around the world?
  • What countries do you associate with the term "banana republic"?
  • Why do you think the US and the EU disagree about the banana market?

2 Now read the text below and choose the correct alternative to fill each gap.

"What's in a bunch of bananas?"

The original "banana republics" are to be found in Central America where most of the world's banana exports come from. In (1) _____, bananas are produced in a number of former French and British colonies in the Caribbean. Even though the (2) _____ are considerably more expensive than the former (40%), a number of European nations have been reluctant to abandon their traditional supplier and have even (3) _____ import quotas for what they call "dollar bananas". Germany, (4) _____, has no traditional ties to the West Indies and has always opted for free entry for "dollar bananas".

In 1993, the European Commission tried to restrict cheaper "dollar banana" imports mainly (5) _____ it was fairly easy to import these into Germany and then ship them to other parts of the EU to the detriment of the Caribbean producers. There was an outcry in Germany. There is an historic reason for this: (6) _____ to the fall of the Berlin Wall, bananas were a rare luxury in the East. With the disappearance of the wall, they became a symbol of freedom. In the same way, for the Spanish, during and after the Spanish Civil War, bananas symbolised affluence, a respite from the war and the availability of goods.

Germany reluctantly accepted European directives, but the US claimed that the Europeans were not (7) _____ hurting the interests of Central America, but also those of the US corporation the Chiquita Banana Company. The US took the battle to the World Trade Organization almost (8) _____ it was set up. Shortly before the retirement of its first Director General, Renato Ruggiero, in April 1999, the WTO ruled that the EU's banana import regulations were protectionist and needed substantial overhaul.

At the same time the WTO approved the imposition of more than $191 million in sanctions on a range of European products – (9) _____ French handbags and German coffeemakers – to recoup lost revenues. The US had sought sanctions amounting to $520 million and their hit list of European products had ranged from cashmere sweaters to cheese. In Brussels, the EU maintained that the banana policy was there to protect former colonies, (10) _____ the Americans argue that very little of the premium price paid for the Caribbean bananas actually goes back to the growers.

1 a) theory   b) principle   c) addition   d) reality
2 a) latter   b) last   c) Caribbean   d) bananas
3 a) raised   b) imposed   c) promised   d) called
4 a) although   b) contrarily   c) otherwise   d) however
5 a) because of   b) because   c) due to   d) given
6 a) prior   b) before   c) anterior   d) previous
7 a) really   b) justly   c) always   d) only
8 a) instantly   b) when   c) as soon as   d) once
9 a) including   b) such   c) as   d) even
10 a) meantime   b) whereas   c) likewise   d) otherwise

3 Read the following letters to a newspaper. In most of the numbered lines there is
one extra word. Identify the extra words and cross them out.

1 Sir, I am a New Zealander living in Europe. Whenever I go to buy the meat,
2 read about subsidies to farmers or about milk quotas my blood begins to boil
3 over. If European farmers cannot produce at competitive prices then perhaps
4 they should be spend their time doing other things. Why should I pay double
5 when I buy meat? First I pay the shop price, which is considerably more higher
6 than it would be in New Zealand, and in addition, my taxes are used moreover to
7 pay subsidies to the farmers, in theory to keep the price to the consumer down.
8 Meanwhile, if I want to eat New Zealand meat, when I buy it, I know that then
9 a fairly hefty proportion of the end price is duties that have been paid at the point
10 of entry into Europe. If trade were free, if there were no tariffs, I'd be spending on
less for more. Fair prices now!

1 We are a middle-sized European textile company. My father has started the
2 company some fifty years ago. However though, I doubt that my own children will
3 be able to work in the family business. Competition is being too tough. The market
4 is being swamped with cheap products made in developing nations. They come in,
5 in the name of free trade. We are obliged to insure for our employees: health,
6 accident, unemployment and retirement insurance at the least. Yet we are expected
7 to compete against products made in sweat shops, where employees are ever
8 uninsured and work in deplorable conditions for a pittance. Who does free trade
9 protect for? Most certainly not those employees. Nor us. Does it then protect the
10 consumer? I doubt it. Who is responsible for faulty goods? Does free trade really
guarantee fair trade?

4 Compare the opinions expressed in the letters and discuss which one is closer to
your own view. Give reasons for your opinions.

C Speaking and writing

Attracting foreign investment

Complete the text using the correct form of the words in brackets. The first one has been done for you.

In order to attract foreign _investment_ (invest), governments and local bodies often offer special conditions such as attractive (1) _____ (subsidise) to those companies wishing to set up in their country or area. (2) _____ (generosity) start-up packages, which (3) _____ (inclusion) tax holidays – in other words, no tax (4) _____ (pay) for the first few years, tax relief, which means (5) _____ (reduce) tax rates if certain conditions are (6) _____ (meeting), and other incentives draw potential investors. But this is not always enough, particularly for (7) _____ (manufacture). To attract them, governments themselves also need to spend large sums of money on (8) _____ (improvement) infrastructures, creating (9) _____ (industry) parks and training future (10) _____ (employ).

1 A multinational wants to analyse where the company should manufacture abroad. A number of key factors are taken into account. These include:

a) the political situation
b) the economic situation
c) the location and infrastructure
d) the labour market
e) the conditions offered to foreign investors

Look at the questions below. Which factor (a–e) do they refer to?

1 Is there free movement of capital and profits for foreign companies or are currency regulations restrictive for everyone? ____

2 Does the government offer any tax incentives to foreign companies? ____

3 How skilled is the workforce? ____

4 Is inflation under control? ____

5 Is there a state-of-the-art telecommunications network? ____

6 Is there any political unrest at all? ____

7 Is there much state intervention or has the economy been liberalised? ____

8 What are wages like in comparison to neighbouring countries? ____

9 Is the country well placed to access target markets? ____

10 Are there high social welfare costs? ____

2 What else is important? In pairs, make up questions to ask about other factors such as:

- economic growth (sustained, rapid or slow)
- consumer purchasing power
- language skills
- incentives for expansion of the company

3 In pairs, answer the questions in 1 and 2 about your own country and talk about why your country is attractive to invest in.

4 This role play is for two speakers.

Chapman Dunne's is an Australian biscuit manufacturer. The company is considering setting up a factory closer to their growing Eastern European and Middle East markets. The company will need to have expatriate technical and managerial staff working in the new factory for the first few years at least.

A and B are directors who have been asked to investigate where the company could or should build the new plant. The company's priorities are:

- strategic location (in terms of services and transport links)
- generous government support
- ample labour supply
- secure investment

Compare the two countries, Arkland and Vilivia, and talk about the advantages each has to offer and any drawbacks that might influence the company's decision.

A looks at this page. B turns to page 79.

SPEAKER A

	Arkland	Vilivia
Political situation	• democratic government • social welfare state • strict controls on manufacturing processes (especially health, safety and environmental issues)	
Economic situation	• sustained economic growth • long industrial tradition • small domestic market • pro-business environment	
Location and infrastructure	• easy access to European and Middle Eastern markets • well-serviced industrial estates • excellent transport infrastructure	
Labour market	• well-trained, skilled workforce • strict labour laws • competitive labour costs	
Conditions for foreign investors	• generous government support (tax holiday for the first five years, generous tax relief thereafter) • excellent facilities for resident foreigners (schools, etc)	

5 Write a short report, to be presented to the Board of Directors, outlining the advantages and drawbacks of setting up a factory in each country. The report should be organised as follows:

PURPOSE   The purpose of this report is to ...

BACKGROUND   Over the last few years there has been considerable growth in ...

OPTIONS ANALYSED   In each case we have investigated the following factors: strategic location, government support, labour supply, investment risk

RECOMMENDATION   Based on the factors considered above, we now make the following recommendations ...

The bottom line

comparing and contrasting

exchanging information about figures

discussing problems and solutions

KEY VOCABULARY

Accounting and taxation

Match the expressions on the left with the definitions on the right.

1 bookkeeping
2 deferral
3 flat fee
4 liquidity
5 loophole
6 off-shore company
7 PAYE (Pay As You Earn)
8 surcharge
9 VAT (Value Added Tax)
10 write off

A a charge that always stays the same
B an additional cost or supplement
C available cash, or assets which can be readily converted into cash
D cancel, deduct, remove the value of an asset in a company's accounts
E a company based in another country (often a tax haven with low taxes) for taxation purposes
F an income tax system, levied as a pro rata percentage of salaries, wages, etc and deducted from the gross salary
G a legal means of evading a law or rule (eg tax legislation)
H the postponement of payment
I the recording of accounts payable and received
J UK sales tax, imposed as a percentage on the invoice of goods and services

A Reading

1 Look at the home page of a tax consultancy firm. In each sentence (1–10) there is one wrong word. Underline the word and write the correct word in the space.

George and Baird Tax Consultants **The Taxation Experts**

Paying More Tax Than You Need To? You Need Us!

Taxes are possibly the most universally unliked of all personal and company finance matters.   _disliked_

1. Good tax advise can save money.   _____

2. At George and Baird, we take proud in the success of our tax minimisation strategies.   _____

3. Our expertise and customised software can maximise your annual tax bill accurately and speedily.   _____

4. Our tax advisors can help you to make the most of tax deferral and another legitimate actions to reduce your tax bill.   _____

5. Maximise what you can legally write off and take advantage on tax incentives and relief. _____

6. Our expert team can find everything loophole in the system.   _____

7. Work with experts in wealthy management and taxation.   _____

8. Learn how to deploy off-shore companies and tax heavens.   _____

9. Keep up to date on special advantages and opportunities been offered abroad.   _____

10. Fees are charge either as a commission on actual tax savings or as a flat fee for on-going consultation.   _____

FAQ

Rights

Confidentiality

Services

Contact us

2 The text below comes from an advice column in a business magazine. Choose the correct alternative to fill each gap.

ACCORDING TO ANALYSTS, many businesses run into liquidity problems simply because of a lack of planning. (1) _____ the widespread use of information systems, far too many companies, they say, are unaware (2) _____ the real profit/loss situation (commonly known as the bottom line) of their business until a crisis rears its ugly head. Far too often in smaller companies budgets are associated with bureaucracy or are considered to be time-consuming and therefore do not even exist.

To be forewarned is to be forearmed: budgeting is, in fact, a useful planning (3) _____. If a business makes a forecast, then a comparison of real activity with forecast activity paves the way for early identification of (4) _____ spots or difficulties and as such, appropriate action can be (5) _____ in time. The differences encountered may, of course, be due to an unrealistic appreciation of the market. In this case, having worked (6) _____ an operating budget and being able to compare it with the real world may dampen spirits, but it will give the business the opportunity to get back on the right track, diverting its energy into areas of growth.

Taxes due should form part and parcel of an operating budget. In most (if not all) countries, revenue commissioners (7) _____ a hard line with businesses or individuals that pay late or incorrectly. Why pay a hefty surcharge if you can (8) _____ it through planning? Some taxes (like VAT and PAYE deductions) have to be paid regularly, so the corresponding amounts should figure in the budget. Good budgeting and bookkeeping can (9) _____ the tax burden considerably. Adequate planning and keeping records means having information, and therefore control. A business in control will (10) _____ everything it can and therefore pay to the tax department what is strictly payable and no more than that.

1 a) Regardless b) Despite c) Although d) Even
2 a) of b) in c) off d) for
3 a) formula b) tool c) lever d) paper
4 a) pitfall b) difficulty c) complex d) trouble
5 a) made b) making c) taken d) taking
6 a) up b) out c) over d) in
7 a) take b) make c) draw d) go
8 a) help b) escape c) cancel d) avoid
9 a) lighter b) lighten c) alight d) alighten
10 a) deduct b) cut c) write down d) underwrite

3 In pairs, talk about the following:
- What experience have you had with budgets?
- Why are the words budget and taxation unattractive to many people?
- Give reasons for and advantages of contracting a tax specialist.

B Listening

Join the sentence halves, using *that, when, where, which, who* or *whose* to complete the definitions.

1 A revenue commissioner is a person
2 A high net worth individual is a person
3 A third party is a person, company or organisation
4 An audit takes place
5 An automatic teller is a machine in a bank
6 Double bookkeeping is a system of accounting
7 Tax evasion occurs
8 The OECD (Organisation for Economic Co-operation and Development) is an organisation

A accounts are officially examined.
B aim it is to encourage and develop economic and social policy.
C has many more assets than liabilities, ie is rich.
D involves having two sets of accounts, only one of which is declared to tax authorities.
E is not one of the main interested parties in a contract or relationship.
F job it is to examine tax returns and determine how much tax must be paid.
G people or companies use illegal means to avoid paying taxes.
H dispenses money to clients when a special card is used and instructions are followed.

1 ⊙ Listen to Part 1 of an interview with a revenue commissioner. Mark the statements true or false.

1 If the tax department wants to find out whether someone can afford to buy an expensive car, they can get this information by analysing data stored in a computer. T F
2 Spot audits determine whether outside information received matches what has been declared. T F
3 Only banks give information to the Inland Revenue Department. T F
4 In-depth investigations tend to affect companies more than individual citizens. T F
5 If one company has taken over another there is more likely to be an investigation. T F
6 At one stage or another 40 per cent of the population will be subject to a thorough tax audit. T F

2 ⊙ Now listen to Part 2 of the interview and choose the correct alternative to complete the sentences.

1 Tax evasion _____.

   a) is easier to control than it used to be
   b) has diversified and become more complex
   c) is more professional than it used to be

2 Globalisation of the economy has _____.

   a) made tax inspection more complex
   b) made tax inspection impossible
   c) divided tax inspection into countries

3 The globalisation of the economy means _____.

   a) countries will have to co-operate more in the future
   b) inland revenue departments will have to begin to co-operate
   c) inland revenue departments will have to get better

3 Listen again and take notes about what is said regarding:

    a) the past

    b) the present

    c) the future

    of tax inspection services. Then discuss what you think will or should happen.

KEY VOCABULARY

Complete the phrases below using the verbs in the box. There may be more than one possible verb.

achieve	call	file	handle	keep	make	reach	submit

1 _____ a report

2 _____ a tender

3 _____ tight control

4 _____ an objective

5 _____ for bids

6 _____ forecasts

7 _____ problems

8 _____ sales targets

4 🎧 Budgets play a key role in business. You are going to hear five extracts. In each one a person comments on the budgeting procedure in his/her place of work. Before you listen, discuss how budgets can be controlled and how important this is.

Then listen and identify which sector the speaker works for. Choose from options A–H.

1 ____

2 ____

3 ____

4 ____

5 ____

A agriculture
B banking
C construction
D chemicals
E health
F information technology
G metalworking
H textiles

5 Match each extract with **one** of the opinions below. Which speaker …

    a) believes that the system leads to poorer service? ____

    b) feels that goal-driven budgeting creates tension? ____

    c) has to control the budget as work progresses? ____

    d) is very happy with the new system of budgeting? ____

    e) says that a problem was highlighted recently? ____

    f) thinks that the current system is obsolete? ____

C   Speaking and writing

Exchanging information about figures

Match the questions on the left with the answers on the right.

1 Are we managing to keep maintenance costs down?

2 How are we doing with general expenses? Are we over or under budget?

3 How much have we spent so far on wages and salaries?

4 Has income from non-member fees gone up?

5 How much did we receive in course fees?

6 Did we manage to cut back on publicity?

A Although we've kept overtime hours down, expenditure has gone up a little.

B Not quite as much as we'd expected, I'm afraid.

C We're doing quite well, really. They've fallen more than 5 per cent.

D Yes, it has, it's gone up nearly 5 per cent. More of them have come this season.

E Yes, we're nearly 5 per cent below budget.

F Yes, we did. We're nearly 25 per cent below budget.

1 This role play is for two speakers.

Situation

The Barot Centre is a sports and leisure complex. As local government subsidies are unlikely to be guaranteed in the future, the centre's management has taken certain decisions in order to increase income and reduce expenditure.

The caterers, who run the centre's bar and restaurant, are now paying a significantly higher rent in exchange for being able to organise private functions (eg parties) when the centre is otherwise closed. The centre itself has also started to rent out facilities to other user groups (eg schools, youth clubs).

In order to save money, the centre has changed a number of suppliers (cleaning, security, telephone).

Everyone is aware that these policies have not been entirely successful. Vandalism has occurred and club members have complained about damaged or missing equipment and the lower standard of cleanliness.

The Managing Director has requested a full report on the current situation.

A is the Facilities Director at the centre. B is in charge of administration. A and B have to prepare for a budget committee meeting to assess performance to date.

A only has figures regarding the use of facilities. B has some of the other figures. Prepare the questions you are going to ask each other to obtain the missing information. The *Key expressions* above will help you.

When you are both ready, A phones B. A looks at this page. B turns to page 82.

SPEAKER A

Barot Centre: Budget Jan–Mar (euros)

	Budget	Actual	Difference	%
INCOME				
Membership fees	502,000			
Non-member fees	19,600			
Special course fees	130,000			
Rental of equipment, towels, etc	2,000	1,320	–680	–34%
Rental of facilities†	8,300	14,350	+6,050	+73%
Subsidies, grants, fundraising††	22,000	4,250	–15,750	–71.6%
TOTAL INCOME	683,900			
EXPENDITURE				
Furniture, fittings, equipment	24,200	32,357	+8,157	+33.7%
General expenses (heating, water, lighting, phone, etc)	44,250			
Maintenance: facilities/equipment	24,300	23,100	–1,200	–4.9%
Cleaning*	41,500	43,500	+2,000	+4.8%
General administrative overheads (postage, stationery, IT, etc)	1,600			
Publicity	18,540			
Professional services, security, etc	30,800			
Salaries (gross)	376,535			
Financial overheads, tax**	115,480	114,427	–1,053	–0.9%
TOTAL EXPENDITURE	677,205			
BALANCE	+4,695			

†good publicity has attracted many outsiders   ††government subsidies – not paid yet
*vandalism, cleaning, etc – not enough security?   **provisional: data supplied by accountant

2 This role play is for two speakers.

A meeting has been called to discuss the budget. Play the same role as in Exercise 1.
Using the information on your role card in Exercise 1, discuss:
• the causes underlying the current situation
• the future implications of the current situation
• possible courses of action

A looks at this page. B turns to page 82.

3 The Managing Director has asked for a quarterly budget report. Use the information gathered in the role play to write a report of about 200–250 words about the current situation. Include a brief introduction, an assessment, and provisional recommendations.

Role play: Speaker B/C/D

Look at the advertisement and decide which characteristics you are going to be looking for and how you are going to ask about them. The first few minutes are vital, so make sure you and the candidate are relaxed.

The job pays an above-average salary and there are many bonus factors depending on experience, performance, punctuality, the need to travel, etc. The company has flexible working hours and employees take days off in lieu of overtime. Promotion prospects are excellent for the right candidate.

You need to:
• find out whether the candidate can work independently as well as in a team
• be convinced by the candidate's ability to perform
• find out when the candidate can begin (your client would prefer someone who can start just after the summer holidays, but would be willing to come into the company, unpaid, for a couple of days prior to this date)

PRESS CONFERENCE FACT SHEET
Zara International

ORIGINS
Zara or **Zara International** is the flagship of **Inditex**, a group made up of 60 different companies, not all of which are in textiles. The company, whose major shareholder is Amancio Ortega, started up as a manufacturer of _____ in 1963 in _____, Spain. It operated initially out of a small workshop. So successful was this first venture that Ortega left his job with a shirt company and expanded the business. During the economic slump in the early seventies he bought out ailing textile manufacturers and set up Inditex. The first Zara outlet opened in _____.

FIGURES
Outlets: Every fortnight a new Zara shop opens up somewhere in the world. (1998 figures)
The group had 24 outlets in 1985, _____ in 1996, 652 in 1997 and 740 (483 in Spain, 257 elsewhere) in _____.
Average investment per outlet was 3 million euros.
The **annual turnover** in 1985 was 30 million euros; in 1997 it was 1.12 billion euros and in _____ 2.03 billion euros.

The group generates a daily **net profit** of more than 0.4 million euros. Between 1994 and 1999 sales _____ and net profit tripled.
The group employed 11,000 people in 1996; 12,000 in 1997.

Distribution: Orders are met within two weeks. A fleet of more than _____ trucks plus several company aircraft distribute new merchandise twice weekly to the stores. Warehouses are emptied three times more often than the sector average.

SALES
55% Spain, 33% Europe, 8% Latin America, 4% rest of the world

FUTURE PLANS
The company aims to create a retail network across Europe. They plan to open _____ new stores over the next three years and forecast a 25 per cent increase in turnover.

UNIT 3
SPEAKER B

- Return A's greeting. Welcome A to the fair/stand/city, etc.
- A will ask for a catalogue. Hand it over enthusiastically. Ask A about his/her line of business. Start generating interest in the product/service.
- Present your product.
- Offer to send information and suggest a meeting.
- Agree the day/time of the meeting.

UNIT 5
SPEAKER B

The Olive Shop (established 2000)

A chain of stores where everything you can make from olives and olive trees can be found: oil, olives, scented oil, soap, cakes, sauces, preserves, furniture, accessories. Possibility of further expansion by franchising stores. The third outlet is about to open.

Investment: 100,000 euros per wholly-owned outlet
Jobs: three per outlet plus 20 in HQ
Return on investment: current net profit 15 per cent p.a.

SPEAKER C

Business start-up: Sweet Sleepers

A store full of products to help you and your dear ones to sleep better. Bed linen, beds, pillows, herbal dispensers, anti-snoring devices and remedies are just a few of our star products.

Initial investment: 100,000 euros   Jobs: two (shop), three (IT/office)
Projected turnover: 500,000 euros p.a.   Return on investment: 15–25 per cent p.a.
Running costs: 225,000 euros p.a.   Plans to expand on-line and via franchise

SPEAKER D

Business start-up: Ingredients.com

An on-line database giving subscribers precise data on what they are eating: genetically modified products, additives, what's in the vegetable oil, the food chain. Essential for people with allergies. Links to suppliers.

Initial investment: 100,000 euros   Expected website hits per day: 50,000+
Running costs: 1,000,000 euros p.a.   Projected turnover: 1.2m euros (year 1)
Jobs: 30   Return on investment: 50–100 per cent p.a.

CASE STUDY

Background: a major motor vehicle manufacturer with well over average number and frequency of medical claims, injuries to shoulders, forearms, back, etc; 150+ working days lost/month in instrument panel selection division

Solutions:
- workstations redesigned
- extra conveyor belts installed
- two specially designed handling devices installed
- staff awareness programme set up

Results: estimated savings: direct wages 80,000 euros, medical costs 34,000 euros p.a. (cost of ergonomics operation: 100,000 euros, including new equipment)

Future plans: company has requested proposal for other sections, including administration

UNIT 7

SPEAKER B

You are interested in reaching an agreement with Sauberlink as they would be a solid, solvent regular customer and could help to build your growing reputation as a friendly restaurant where the food is excellent and the prices reasonable. Lunchtimes are very busy, so you would like to ensure the following:

Food:
A minimum of two days' notice when special menus are requested. (What specialities can you offer? Can you offer anything else, eg music?)
A minimum of four people (a maximum of 12) if the private dining room is required (if fewer people come, there will be a surcharge – how much?).

Scheduling:
Punctuality is important to ensure optimal organisation of space, staff and the kitchen. (How will you deal with cancellations? What happens if they arrive late? Could they come before/after the peak period?)

Price:
The average price of a quality menu is 20 euros, without beverages; 30 euros including beverages (mark-up is 100 per cent on beverages, 10–40 per cent on food).
The quality of the food and service are key factors when building a reputation and you do not want to lower these.

Another point:
Sauberlink has a showroom where they hold a variety of events at the off-peak time of the day (for restaurants). You would like to cater for these functions.

UNIT 8
PAIR B

Chasers Sports Shoes have been boycotted worldwide because of reports that they employ children in their factories.

Key events:

August: A well-known magazine publishes an article in which Chasers is accused of using child labour in the manufacturing of their sports shoes.

August: The company denies this information categorically and files a lawsuit.

October: A television documentary depicts child labour manufacturing worldwide.

October: A campaign against Chasers is launched on the internet.

November: A press conference is called by Chasers denying the accusations. Christmas campaign begins with a positive-sounding message.

Possible strategies:

- Investigate which sector has stopped buying shoes and what would convince them to buy Chasers products again. Act upon information obtained. *(will be time-consuming)*
- Sign up key sports personalities to endorse products. *(can be very expensive)*
- Continue to send out positive messages about production methods (especially if the Christmas campaign is effective).
- Sponsor key charity events.
- Provide incentives to distribution outlets to promote the products. *(lower profit margin)*
- Provide free products/vouchers/competition entry forms for every pair of Chasers shoes purchased.
- Target the internet-user market with assertive publicity.

Chasers sales — Sales (1,000 pairs): 0, 10, 20, 30, 40; months Jan–Dec; last year / this year

UNIT 11
SPEAKER B

	Arkland	Vilivia
Political situation		• unstable government • frequent cases of civil unrest
Economic situation		• no restrictions on movement of capital profits and dividends • growth economy • no price controls • high inflation
Location and infrastructure		• modern infrastructure • 21st century telecommunications • large domestic market, close to major European and Middle Eastern markets • supportive environment for business development (new business parks, etc)
Labour market		• abundant workforce at relatively low cost
Conditions for foreign investors		• attractive investment packages with tax holidays and other incentives • few international schools, hospitals, etc

Appolinus

Background information:

- You have a longstanding, very solid business relationship with Sanicui.
- You are currently importing active ingredients used in an anti-viral treatment formula from Peru. Supplies are en route and should arrive within a week. They have been delayed because of adverse weather conditions.
- You have been having difficulties with your internet link and have not been able to keep customers informed as usual.
- Sanicui have placed and urgent order with you. However, according to your calculations Sanicui should have two weeks' supplies left. Have they been selling in other countries where the profit margin is higher? (You have an agreement that this is not allowed.)

Remember:

- You based your orders on national health forecasts and these were correct (so why is there a shortage?).
- Company policy is not to pay extra costs for emergency supplies, unless shortages have been caused by Appolinus (or the client is a very valued customer).
- Solutions can always be found, but there is a price (try to increase your margins).

Options:

Source	Lead time	Cost difference	Observations
Peru	3–4 weeks	current supplier	Order is en route; if cancelled, what will you do with unused stocks? cancellation fee = 30%
Brazil	3 days	+15–18%	Minimum order = 50% of current Appolinus order
Colombia	2 days or 4 days	+25% or +15%	
Other	Synthetic substitutes available + 32% cost, minimum 3 days' lead time		

According to your information, Sanicui has the following options:

Source	Lead time	Cost difference	Observations
Salutus	2–4 days	+20%	Large minimum orders (how much?)
Rival laboratories in other countries	2–4 days	+35–50%	Any business relationships established?

Sanicui will now call you.

UNIT 10
SPEAKER B

Human resources

Main problems:

- staff undervalued
- staff knowledge under-exploited
- staff under-trained

Solutions:

- set up regular re-training to keep staff up-to-date (making them a real asset to customers)
- train staff as information-gatherers for: a) customer feedback, b) customer complaints and c) customer suggestions
- create a system to process and act on information and suggestions from staff
- set up staff awards to encourage positive participation

SPEAKER C

Information technology

Main problems:

- the company's internal computer system (the company has computerised its supply chain very successfully, but its own intranet is inefficient)
- poor information flow between departments within the company
- staff are not skilled at information-sharing (resulting in duplication of effort)
- the possibilities of on-line sales have not been exploited

Solutions:

- redesign software for the intranet to improve information flow between the store and the offices
- run team-building programmes (starting at the top)
- create on-line solutions for customers (ordering, delivering and giving information about products, etc)

SPEAKER D

Management and team-building

Main problems:

- old-fashioned, hierarchical managerial style
- communication flow between management and staff is poor
- management think "they know best" and make changes without consulting the market

Solutions:

- re-engineer the company
- create new software, so that informed decision-making can take place
- run team-building seminars to change the managerial mind-set

Barot Centre: Budget Jan–Mar (euros)

	Budget	Actual	Difference	%
INCOME				
Membership fees	502,000	502,000	=	=
Non-member fees	19,600	20,480	+880	4.5%
Special course fees	130,000	128,500	−1,500	−1.15%
Rental of equipment, towels, etc	2,000			
Rental of facilities	8,300			
Subsidies, grants, fundraising	22,000			
TOTAL INCOME	683,900			
EXPENDITURE				
Furniture, fittings, equipment	24,200			
General expenses (heating, water, lighting, phone, etc)	44,250	41,750	−2,500	−5.6%
Maintenance: facilities/equipment	24,300			
Cleaning	41,500			
General administrative overheads (postage, stationery, IT, etc)[†]	1,600	4,450	+2,850	+178%
Publicity[††]	18,540	14,200	−4,340	−23.4%
Professional services, security, etc[*]	30,800	20,300	−10,500	−34%
Salaries (gross)	376,535	379,308	+2,773	+0.7%
Financial overheads, tax[**]	115,480	114,427	−1,053	−0.9%
TOTAL EXPENDITURE	677,205			
BALANCE	+4,695			

[†] IT maintenance up on account of problems – staff had to work overtime   [††] have cut back on advertising

[*] cost-cutting effective – eg new security service employed (33% cheaper)   [**] provisional: data supplied by accountant

Tapescript

Part B

Exercises 1 and 2

I = interviewer
RO = recruitment officer

I   And today's special guest on "The World's Your Oyster" is a recruitment officer from one of our country's leading financial institutions. A lot of young people are out there looking for a job. How many people does your bank recruit annually?

RO   Normally the National Westminster Bank Group is looking for about 200 graduate management trainees each year: people they expect to become managers and senior managers in the medium term.

I   In the medium term – how long is that?

RO   Well, it takes at least ten years to get to be a proper manager, and you're talking about a career which will last until retirement, in many cases. But the NatWest, as we call the National Westminster Bank, doesn't just recruit this group of 200. It also recruits around about twenty, what are called "super grads".

I   Pardon? Super what?

RO   Super grads means super graduates. People who we think have the potential to become chief executive, deputy chief executive, general manager at the height of their career. NatWest also recruits at a lower level. We recruit graduates who don't want the pressure that a graduate manager trainee scheme will involve. We're looking for about fifty of these graduates each year.

I   Who else do you recruit?

RO   We're also looking for people who, twenty years ago, we would have got from the 18-year-old school leaver market. These days most 18-year-olds who have been to a reasonable school can go to a university, and many do so.

I   Is this recruitment system fairly standard?

RO   Well, yes, there are other companies with similar systems. Ford Motor Company have their equivalent of the super grad scheme, as do other companies, because we're all looking for people to be senior executives at some stage in the future.

I   Can you give the young people listening today an idea about the sort of people you're looking for?

RO   Well, basically, we're looking for people who can be managers, who can manage people, and can be salesmen and can do all sorts of different jobs. We're not necessarily looking for people who've got first-class honours degrees; we're looking for the graduate who is also involved in union activities, sports activities, other social activities at university. The actual degree subject is of no consequence whatsoever. There's no proof that any one subject of degree leads to greater or lesser success.

I   How do you go about recruiting potential employees?

RO   We send them an application form, and we agree to see students on what's called the "milk round" in the UK. This is the period between March – January to March – when all the employers of any size visit the universities to carry out preliminary interviews. But not everyone who submits an application form gets an interview. There is pre-selection.

I   And how is pre-selection done?

RO   Pre-selection involves a graduate recruitment team. In the case of NatWest, it means a team of three, looking at the forms and saying, "This is of interest," or "That is not of interest," and out of the 5,000 application forms which are received, NatWest will probably arrange to do a first interview for about 2,000 students.

I   From 5,000 to 2,000 – that's a sizeable reduction. On what basis do you make your decisions?

RO   On the basis of the other things they've done. Do they look as if they're going to be interesting individuals? *[HuhHuh.]* In a bank like NatWest, we don't want people who have brilliant results but have never seen the light of day, have never been involved with people, and are not commonsense people. So when NatWest are doing

pre-selection and when the other banks are looking, they're looking for the same sort of generalised good performance, both on the academic and the social side. The more social things that have been done, often, the better.

Exercises 5 and 6

1   Well, I've applied for this job because I really feel that I have the skills and experience you're looking for. As you can see from my CV, my experience is quite varied, and as I'm working in a smallish company I have to co-ordinate a variety of areas at the same time, particularly when my boss is away on business, which is quite often. I end up bearing a fair bit of responsibility and I've learnt to deal with all sorts of people, calls and circumstances. Of course, bookkeeping, correspondence and information technology are part and parcel of my everyday life. After all, the basic job is quite paperwork-oriented. Yes, I'm proficient in all three areas …

2   Good morning. I'm calling on behalf of HTT regarding your job application. *[pause]* I'm pleased to be able to tell you that we have short-listed you for an interview. *[pause]* Now I need a few more details regarding your résumé, and when you come, you'll need to bring in proof of your foreign language skills and any letters of reference you have, both character reference and professional, if you can. *[pause]* Can you also get a job description of your current post to us so that we can ask pertinent questions? *[pause]* On paper it would seem that you have enough relevant systems experience, and during the selection procedure you'll be given an opportunity to demonstrate that, um …

3   Yes, I'd like some information about the job advertised on the employment service notice board. *[pause]* It's MSA 3011. *[pause]* That's right … Um, do you know the company's website address? I'd like to find out about them as well. *[pause]* Thank you. Do you know if there'll be a training period and how long and when this will take place? You see, I'm on this really very good course on innovative cyber-marketing and I'd hate to have to drop out, but … *[pause]* What was that? Selection normally takes a couple of months or so? Great. What stages are there? *[pause]* Uh huh, maths test, compatibility, group dynamics … yeah, yeah. Oh, by the way, have they mentioned anything about pay, hours and conditions? *[pause]* No, I have no real experience …

Part B

Exercises 1 and 2

1   When we started out, back in 1951, there were three owners and six employees, and we were manufacturing battery terminals. Soon afterwards we diversified production to include a range of items and, at the time, we were supplying the automobile and household appliance sectors. By the 1970s we were no longer supplying the latter but already had a staff of 1,500. We decided to sell out to a multinational and we haven't stopped growing since. We now have our own R&D centre, employing 200 people; employee numbers have risen to around 5,000, and turnover has gone up ten-fold. Seventy-five per cent of our production currently goes to Germany, Sweden, France, Spain, Belgium and England, mainly to vehicle manufacturers. We were recently praised by the unions for our safety record …

2   Our company was founded over forty years ago by a miller's son who had moved to the city to set up a business making a variety of pastries and cakes. A year after his arrival, in 1962, this same man, the father of our present owner, made a trip to the USA and brought back a souvenir, a round pastry with a hole in the middle. Nobody really knows if he'd already thought about actually making them or whether the reaction of his children to this souvenir, the donut, did the trick, but that event changed everything. Our company now makes more than 700 million of them a year. We sell from 80,000 sales points and have never once had any legal claims made regarding freshness and quality. In fact, freshness is our hallmark. Recently we entered into a joint venture with our major outside shareholder to set up and supply Dunkin' Donuts. Now, before we go …

3 I have a client, Pat, whose company started out doing very well. Pat's strategy was to recruit top agents. It worked. Clients regarded the staff as being knowledgeable, friendly and extremely professional. The company attracted both property owners wishing to lease premises and solvent tenants wanting to rent. He ended up with more business than he could really cope with. But instead of growing gradually with the demand, Pat decided to double the size of his business, just like that. He leased larger premises and started to employ staff to fill them. People didn't want to work for him because he seemed too eager to employ them and much the same happened with clients. People didn't trust him and he lost out. He lost clients, he lost employees, he lost the chance to grow. What he should have done was …

4 When you look at our star product – award-winning universal remote control units, which compete with Asian-made products – it seems hard to believe that we started out, in the late 1950s, making buttons and plastic packaging. The main transformation and most crucial growth period in the company occurred between 1985 and 1990. We realised that competing with the giants was a lost cause. We didn't want to sell out and our most viable alternative was to work with them instead. Apart from the remote control units, we also design and make plastic shells for printers and other machines; we work in the area of electronic and mechanical circuits, mould design and so on. We apply the notion of *kaizen* to manufacturing: that's a Japanese word meaning refinement, by doing little things better.

5 We started out as a quiet affair. I'd inherited a bit of money from a distant relative who'd made it in Australia and I wasn't happy in my job, so my partner and I decided to start up a family-run mini hotel–restaurant with home cooking and so on. We only had four guest rooms and the restaurant was a manageable size, so we didn't need much extra help, initially. Word got around that it was a great place to go. Then we couldn't cope with demand, and we seemed to be paying loads of taxes, so we decided to expand. That was a mistake – we just weren't up to managing staff, keeping quality levels, and handling debt. We sold up for a good price but it's sad, really; we might start again, but it'll stay small next time.

Exercise 3

1 Well, our share of the market is down somewhat this year, but we hope to be able to get back on the right track with the help of our reorganised sales team. We're well below our target 20 per cent and we'll have to work together to bring things back to where they were three years ago.

2 Two years ago growth was at a rate of a new outlet per month. Last year the rate doubled and in the current year growth is fairly steady. In the coming year a new outlet per week is expected to open.

3 Well, the figures for the year ending have just come in and, great, great … sales have bounced back to around the 20 million tonne mark, which is good news.

4 The application of the co-operative management techniques recommended by the consultants has paid off: the figures for this year show that productivity is up, sales are up, absenteeism is down, and, frankly, that means growth.

5 There are two sides to the results for this quarter. Although sales have increased from 22,000 units to 27,000 units – that's from 13,000 units at the beginning of the year – overhead costs have gone up as well. In fact, the increased sales volume has meant, paradoxically, a reduction in the profitability of our company. This is because growth has required investment …

UNIT 3 Part B

Exercise 2

1 I believe we should be fairly pleased with the results of the fair on the whole. Our stand was well attended. I think our survey of existing and potential partners is worth analysing. Two-thirds said they were more satisfied with the outcome of this type of business venture than they had expected – in terms of profits, ongoing assistance and so on – and nearly a quarter enquired about opening an additional branch. Just under half were concerned about the future of their business and a third felt that the terms of the agreement were too restrictive, as they were not allowed to diversify. Just over a third felt that the royalties were too high. Now royalties are what newcomers were most interested in – 98 per cent in fact; start-up costs – 98 per cent again; data providing proof of the viability of the venture, case studies, that sort of thing – 81 per cent;

financial support – 63 per cent; promotion – 60 per cent; staff training – 52 per cent; innovation – 40 per cent …

2 Are these materials as good as we say? Oh, yes, these materials offer distinct advantages to the end-user and are without a doubt the best option currently available. They've been used in the sector in Australia for well over a decade. How safe are they? Very. As you're probably aware, Australia is a country with very strict building codes and safety regulations. Numerous reports and surveys carried out by architects, engineers and surveyors verify this. There really is no doubt about the quality. They're also environmentally friendly, weather resistant, and great for insulation. And prices are extremely competitive. Come this way and I'll show you what we're talking about.

3 Hello again. Sorry about that interruption. Now, where were we? If you want the same decor wherever you go, that's fine, but depending on the venue, a slight change of image might work better in one country than another … *[pause]* Well, how can I put it? It's important to adapt exhibits to local taste. *[pause]* Well, the sessions don't take that long considering their effect. You know, a surprising number of leading companies have lost contracts because they were insensitive to local tastes, customs and ways of thinking. *[pause]* Well, it all depends on the number of services you require, when, where and for how long. Why don't we arrange a meeting and analyse your needs, then we'll work out a proposal. *[pause]* Oh, no, you're under no obligation whatsoever, the proposal is by no means binding …

4
SC = Siobhan Corrigan
E = exhibitor

SC Good morning.
E Good morning. Welcome to our stand. How can I help you?
SC Can I have a catalogue, please? I seem to have left mine at the hotel.
E Oh, certainly. Here you are. Allow me to show you some of our latest products. We have some very innovative modems and scanners. What line of business are you in?
SC We're in the business of creating and adapting information systems in the utilities sector in developing nations. My name's Siobhan Corrigan and I'm in charge of international business relations at O'Reilly Systems Ltd in Cape Town, South Africa.
E What exactly are you interested in, Ms Corrigan?
SC We're looking for user-friendly micro-computers and accessories which are resistant to variations in temperature, humidity and so on. You see, our customers need to make sure that water consumption is measured correctly and that the data is not lost because humidity has damaged the memory.
E We have some excellent products, and it would be my pleasure to give you a demonstration. If you would like to come this way …

Exercise 3

I = interviewer
XV = Xavier Vidal

I Your job requires you to travel a good deal. How do you prepare for business trips abroad?
XV The important thing about a trip is not the trip per se but, ah, rather, preparing what we call "primary information", before leaving. What does that mean? That means that if you haven't already established … if you don't already have contacts or clients, then you have to look for them via for example the internet, where nowadays you can go through the Yellow Pages of a destination. Or you can look for information by getting in touch with international Chambers of Commerce. Then you set up a database of possible clients and you send them a fax, or e-mail, introducing yourself and your company and later you can call them all and try to make an appointment. It's really important to have done all this research before leaving.
I You go to trade fairs, don't you? How many trade fairs do you go to annually?
XV About four a year.
I And how do they vary from one country to another?
XV Radically. Take organisation, for example. A fair organised in Brazil is not the same as one organised in Amsterdam. In Europe, for example, or in the States, most people who visit the fairs are businesspeople and the fairs are organised by sector. In China, fairs are multi-sector. In such countries, people are thirsty for knowledge – everyone's interested, so you can expect to get visits from

students, teachers and politicians as well as prospective clients. So it's sometimes difficult to find people who are really of interest to the company, who might be good clients in the future. As a result, you end up spending more time and energy in developing countries than in developed ones.

I   What makes a fair worthwhile?

XV It's worth having a stand at a fair when it's in a country where communication with people is difficult. Take China, for example. Communication is difficult because of language and also because of logistics. Potential or existing suppliers and clients may be scattered all over the country and it would take a long time to go and visit them all. In such countries, you really need a meeting point where you can get in touch with clients.

I   What about more developed countries – how are they different?

XV In countries where the market is more developed, it's very clear who the importer is, who is in charge of distribution and who does the installing, so it's far easier. In developing nations there are companies that supposedly do everything – importing, distribution and installation. In reality they may not be proficient in any of these, let alone all of them.

I   Increasingly, products are being sold through the internet, business contacts are established through the net … do you think that trade fairs will disappear in the long run?

XV No, they won't disappear. Their role will change. In fact, it's already begun to change. Trade fairs used to be events where you met new clients or customers, where you launched new products or did PR work. Now, with the increased speed of communication, when people go to a fair, they already know what new products there are – you don't go to launch new products; you go there more for public relations with clients than anything else. You're not there to take new orders or to do market research, but rather to build or maintain a relationship with clients as you could do by taking them out for supper or by going to visit their company. If the market is developed and customer knowledge is extensive, the function of the trade fair changes, so that it's no longer launching new products, but rather pure PR.

UNIT 4   Part A

Exercises 1 and 2

1 I run a golf supplies shop, well, four in fact. When we opened the second store, we realised that we had to computerise the tills, the cash registers differently, mainly so that we could check stock instantly and move stock from one store to another if necessary. If, say, a customer wants a particular type of club which one outlet has run out of, or if, say, we're low on balls and the manufacturer says we'll have to wait another week, with the electronic point of sale system – you know, EPoS – it's quite simple. If stock control is offline, and the tills are not connected, you have to resort to the telephone and that's just not efficient these days. Without EPoS we wouldn't be as efficient and in control …

2 With mad cow disease first, then pig health scares, then the chickens and pigs that had been given contaminated feed, we just felt that we could no longer take any risks. The consumer wanted to know what every single animal had been fed on, where it had been raised and so on. And they had a right to that information. So the government decided to make technology available to us and to subsidise it. Now all our animals are fitted with electronic chips and we know everything about every single one of them – origin, breeding, diet, health and so on.

3 I manage over thirty boutiques, which are divided into a number of chains. We sell mainly to women. In this sector you need to know very fast which items are selling well, which fabrics, colours, sizes and styles. But things are not that simple: the manufacturers and so-called fashion experts can't always predict what will sell and we, the retailers, need IT so that we can have access to reliable, first-hand information to spot trends and move fast. We check about a week after new stock comes in how it's selling and that information gives us negotiating power when dealing with manufacturers … so, for example, if on one item it's the larger sizes rather than the smaller ones that are selling well, then we want more of that size and less of the other.

4 We import tiles, mainly from Italy, Spain and other countries, and we use IT not only in B2B relations and to control stocks but also to collect data on customer feedback. That means the opinions both of the professional tile layers and of the end-user, so that we can gauge results. Now we've developed a type of simulator so that the end-user can envisage what certain tiles are going to look like when they're laid. This allows interior decorators and individual customers to see on the screen

what combinations suit them, the image that's going to be created and so on … a type of virtual reality. It's quite something and it certainly gives us competitive advantage over our rivals, at least for now.

5 For many years now, we've used computers for bookkeeping tasks – paying suppliers for fabrics and finished goods like scarves, shirts and so on, salaries, social security, tax. Then we moved into on-line banking, though we still go and see the bank manager occasionally, particularly when we have to negotiate or renegotiate terms. And now we've got into large-scale stock control, not just day-to-day inventory, which we had a programme for, but much more complex stuff than that. You see, analysts started saying that enormous amounts of stock were being lost through theft, and that 50 per cent was due to inside theft – in other words, staff – and that the textile industry was a prime victim. Now, nobody wants to mistrust employees, but statistics are statistics and we decided to include a loss prevention programme so as to give us peace of mind and to pinpoint any possible source of losses of this nature.

UNIT 4   Part C

Exercise 4

> E = examiner
> LV = Lilian Varela

E   Now, Lilian, it's your turn. Do you need a little more time to think about what you're going to say?

LV No, it's OK.

E   Remember, you only have about a minute for this so don't worry if I interrupt you. Susika, when Lilian has finished speaking, you will be invited to ask a question. OK – you can begin now, Lilian.

LV Thank you. Today I'm going to talk about the characteristics of a good website. First of all, I'm going to mention research I'm familiar with, and then describe my own experience.

For a website to be viable, in economic terms, it must be easy to reach and visited often. If it is not, it will attract neither business nor advertising. Research tells us that content is the biggest drawcard, the biggest attraction. Content is what motivates visitors to return. If the site is attractive, then visitors will want to return, and it's a good idea to change at least some of the content regularly to create and/or sustain interest.

Humour is also an attraction. Here in Brazil, we have some sites that have become famous for their sense of humour and are visited very often. They are updated frequently, which as I mentioned before, motivates people to return to the site. The image is important, too. I think that a good image says more than a thousand words.

The second most important factor is that the site must be user-friendly: it needs to be easy to get around. Once a client has hit your site, you need to keep him or her long enough to be able to promote a few products at the same time. It's important to choose the content very carefully. If you introduce a quiz that requires the visitor to download a variety of programmes first, then unless this software downloads quickly or is useful for other sites, visitors are going to lose interest.

So a third factor is speed. A website that takes a long time to download is demotivating, and you're unlikely to make a return visit. On the contrary, you're more likely to interrupt the visit midstream.

E   Thank you, Lilian. Now, Susika, can you ask Lilian something about what she has just said?

UNIT 5   Part A

Exercises 1 and 2

1 Today we received an application for a loan to pay a customer's annual tax bill. Today is the last day for paying any taxes due, so it's a bit late to ask for a loan for that purpose. The type of loan requested was a five-year loan, but the tax return is done every year, so what's going to happen next year? The repayment capacity in this case was not very clear, because although the customer earns a lot of money, mainly through rents on his properties, his capacity for saving is very limited. He's 66. The guarantees are not really very clear either. Because although the value of his assets is considerable, these properties are owned jointly with other relatives. He's not on good terms with these relatives, so if we wanted to execute our rights over this guarantee, it might not be easy to repossess the properties. So the loan has been denied.

2 A supplier of cartography and information systems equipment, founded in 1993 with three shareholders, all members of the same family, asked for the annual renewal of a credit line of 60,000 euros, which they were given for the first time in 1997. The guarantee is the owners' own property. The company's financial situation is very healthy. The share capital is 40,000 euros. The average balance in the current accounts is 24,000 euros. They use our bank for the bulk of their operations: tax, social security, salaries and so on. The group as a whole has liabilities of 267,856 euros – the mortgage plus the loans and credit lines – against average balances amounting to 410,714 euros. In other words, a company with an excellent credit rating. The application has been approved.

3 A company, an established client in the automobile sector, extremely solvent, with an excellent credit rating, favourable cash flow, balance sheet and growth, applied for a long-term loan. There was one major shareholder, now 70 years old, and the guarantee was part of his shares in the company. Presumably, the bank manager smelt something fishy, otherwise the loan would probably have been granted almost automatically. We ran a series of checks on the company, and we found out that the major shareholder had sold most of his shares to a foreign company. This had happened just after the loan had been applied for. Well, we requested all sorts of details relating to the operation: balance sheets, annual reports, risk ratings, and so on. The documents were fascinating. We didn't authorise the loan, as the company was quite unco-operative when we requested more details about the purpose of the loan and the real guarantees.

4 An apparently very successful youngish executive, the manager of a handful of very fashionable nightlife venues in and around the city, applied to us for a loan to buy a Ferrari. The case made us laugh at first, I suppose because you sort of presume that people who buy Ferraris are rich enough to pay for them in cash. Anyway, this 32-year-old man's declared salary didn't correspond to what was deposited in his account monthly and was too low to finance the monthly instalments. Further investigation showed that he was working for a group of companies which had not been legally registered. I don't know if he bought the car or not, but we didn't finance it anyway.

5 The other day we had to decide on this case. We're talking about a smallish, family-run sign-making factory, employing about 16 people. The factory is located at the rear of a building and they applied for a mortgage to buy premises at the front of the building. Doing so would increase the value of the premises considerably and would also legalise the business, as recent legislation obliges all such factories to have a street entrance. From a financial point of view, the company has not always been healthy. Their current financial overheads are considerable and this mortgage was not going to help them. But as they pointed out, financing the mortgage wouldn't cost much more than paying administrative fines – they had a visit from an inspector recently. Well, since the premises themselves were put up as a guarantee, we decided it was a risk the bank could afford to take.

Exercise 4

I = interviewer
JC = investor

I John, to what extent is it true to say that people speculate on the stock exchange rather than invest to receive a dividend?

JC I think it's absolutely true, and I think it started … well, it's always existed to some extent, people buying and selling shares for capital gains reasons. Certainly, that's how I started. When I first bought a share, for instance, in 1969 or 1970, I never even considered the dividend. I was looking to double my money as quickly as possible. When you work in the City of London, as I did at that stage, I think a lot of people are investing for capital gains reasons.

I And if people do want a regular return, an annual yield on their investment, what should they do?

JC Well, when I looked at what I wanted in terms of a regular income, what I did was to look at buying pension plans and investing small amounts to start with, and no-risk investment products like government bonds.

I Tell me, John, in what ways has the world of investment changed?

JC What has happened, in my view, is that first, with the privatisation of so many nationalised companies and then later, with the development of internet-type companies, people have seen that big

gains are possible. People found, for example, that, if they'd bought British Telecom at the issue price in whenever it was, 1983, then they had made decent money, a considerable amount of money. What we've seen in France, in Germany, in the UK and in other countries, but the UK is the leader in this one, is that more and more companies have been privatised. People have seen, as they did with British Telecom, that if they buy a share today, what is interesting is not the dividend, it's the resale value. Nobody's interested in the dividend. All they're interested in is making money quickly.

I Would you recommend investing in the stock exchange?

JC Investing in the stock exchange really depends on your own risk profile. Some people want no risk; some people want a lot of risk. You're going to have to say to yourself when you're buying a share, "Will it hurt me if it all goes wrong?" The problem we've had for the last eight or ten years is that we've almost always been in a bull market as share prices have continued to go up, and the bubble hasn't burst.

I What will happen if it does burst and we go into a bear market?

JC There are investment managers who've never experienced a bear market and when it comes along it will probably kill them, because they have no idea how to deal with a market in which prices are falling. There are lots of people who've got too much money in risky shares, thinking it's never going to go wrong. It will go wrong. Think back to 1987, to Black Monday, the nineteenth of October. The New York stock exchange lost 25 per cent in one day. Now, if you needed that money on that day or that week, you were in deep trouble and people did get into deep trouble. On the other hand, there are other types of investors out there, and I'm one of them, who actually wait for collapses to invest. The market will eventually come back, so if you invest in a bear market you'll end up making money, and if your money's already there and you don't get anxious and can wait, your shares will eventually recover.

I So the key is …

JC Personally, I've never actually got myself into a position where I will need to sell shares to live or to change my car or to pay for my children's education. Also, I think you need to diversify your investment. There are a lot of people out there who think that stock exchange investing is easy and lucrative. They have everything in there, some have even borrowed to buy shares. When it goes wrong there's going to be a lot of crying, because they won't be able to afford the losses.

UNIT 6 Part A

Exercise 1

I = interviewer
SA = Svend Auken

I What are the major concerns of the consumer these days?

SA Well, as far as the West is concerned, people want information. They want product standards to be subject to strict legislation and they want labels to tell them *everything*. Increasingly they're becoming concerned about pollution and are demanding guarantees from the manufacturer or producer that what they are buying is not damaging the environment.

I How do these demands affect globalised production and trade?

SA Well, people in the West are concerned about a number of issues. A lot of publicity has been given to the erosion of biological diversity and also to the effects that certain practices, such as the use of pesticides, are having on freshwater systems all over the world. People are asking for guarantees that products that are imported have not been produced at the expense of the environment. There's another concern, too. And that is, there is a fairly strong feeling that production in some countries is cheaper, in part, because there is a complete and utter disregard for standards regarding workers' health and safety in the production process.

I But in the West there are fairly strict regulations in force, aren't there?

SA Yes, but they're not the same everywhere. The United States and the European Union have had a full-scale confrontation about the labelling of genetically modified foods, for example. But if you take a look at what the European Union has been doing, then you can glean what may well be the bottom line for the future.

I Can you explain that a little?

SA   Yes. When, in the early eighties, the idea of establishing an open market in Europe was proposed, it became clear that the standards and regulations regarding products and processes would have to be harmonised. At the time, every country had its own set of rules. In the end the concept of an open, internal market has led to tighter environmental policies.

I   Why did that happen?

SA   Because those countries with a greater awareness, if you like, of health, safety and the environment, managed to persuade the others that regulations on these matters were essential if the quality of life for European citizens was to be guaranteed. Now, we think – and I mean, that is the consensus opinion of the European Union – we think that international trade agreements must also go hand in hand with environmental agreements.

I   What's the reaction been on the whole?

SA   Mixed, but unfortunately, not very favourable. On the one hand, countries like the USA will not allow international bodies to dictate to them what is or is not in their best interests when it comes to the environment. And in the developing world, many nations see this insistence on imposing international norms on health, safety and the environment as being just another way of setting up trade barriers.

I   Environmentally friendly production is very expensive, though, isn't it? Can these countries, indeed can the world afford it?

SA   The notion that economic development and the environment are opposed to one another is a myth. At present, a lot of the environmental consequences of production processes are hidden from the end-user in the West, because the environmentally unfriendly production is located in developing nations, and that's very short-sighted. In the long run the inhabitants of these developing nations are also going to demand ecologically friendly production. What we have to do is take steps now, rather than wait until even more damage has been done.

I   For example?

SA   Right now, we know that the amount governments receive in taxes and so on from transportation doesn't cover the real cost – and I'm talking here about the cost of its impact on the environment – by a long way. In some cases, at a national level, taxes have been raised to this end, but internationally, we're nowhere near covering the cost. And some day that will have to change …

Exercise 2

I = interviewer
TD = Tom Dwyer

I   I know it's all in your book, but can you describe some cases of industrial accidents and how they might have been avoided?

TD   Well, it's common to see accidents occurring at three levels. One is called organisation, another is called command, another is called reward. Let's take an example of an accident at the organisational level – a nuclear accident, Three Mile Island. What happened there was that you had a system that was of such complexity that the people who were running it couldn't work out what was going on, when things started to go wrong and the plant started leaking. The systems were interlinked in such a way that the operators couldn't understand intuitively what was going on and were unable to take appropriate measures.

I   How could that have been avoided?

TD   The first lesson is: when you build a system, you have to make sure that it is intuitively understandable: operators need to know what to press in the case of an emergency. It's like your computer – you need to be able to shut it down without losing everything. There are many, many cases of accidents that happen in high technology industries because of the way that the systems are constructed.

I   Do other types of accidents occur at this level?

TD   Oh yes, there are accidents at the organisational level in all kinds of sectors. Lack of training is one cause. Disorganisation of work is another. Let's take a case of disorganisation on a construction site. When you put one worker above another on a construction site, you're asking for trouble. Because if the one who's above drops something, it may fall on the person who's below. So the way to avoid that is to put something between the two workers, which is what safety platforms are for, to separate the workers.
Another thing that occurs at the organisational level is monotony, excessive routine work. You repeat and repeat and repeat your tasks and suddenly something goes wrong and you keep on repeating an action that is not appropriate. The way to avoid that is job rotation.

I   The second level you mentioned was the command level. Can you elaborate on that a little?

TD   The Chernobyl nuclear accident was a typical command-level accident. Some people from Moscow wanted to conduct some safety experiments in the Chernobyl plant. They couldn't do it during the day because the people who were in charge were powerful enough to say "no" to them. So they went into the plant at night time, when the top bosses were away and they then had more authority than those in charge at the time. They were senior civil servants. And they ordered people around and started a safety experiment that turned into a nuclear disaster. Authoritarianism produced that accident.

I   And what about command accidents in other sectors?

TD   Well, take the case of people working together when they don't understand each other well. A good case of this can be found in construction sites again. Imagine you have two workers who speak different languages, one an immigrant worker, the other a local worker and they're carrying, let's say, a door. They're walking along a floor and the floor has a hole in it. The first worker can see the hole and step over it. Now if that worker is unable to convey to the second worker that there's a hole there, the second worker is quite possibly going to fall into the hole. This is a typical accident due to lack of communication. Lack of communication within a work group is responsible for something like 8–10 per cent of all accidents.

I   Goodness! What about the reward level then?

TD   The reward level. Here again you have two typical types of accidents. One: accidents linked to piece-working, where you pay per number of items produced. This motivates people to work faster or to work more dangerously. If those payments weren't there, people would be more careful, but people work faster than they know is safe to earn more money, and they end up having accidents. Another example at the reward level is the case of excessive overtime. We have studies showing that people working ten or twelve hours a day have a larger number of accidents – not in all sectors, but in a number – than people who work eight or nine hours a day. Truck drivers, for example. A lot of truck drivers work very long hours, fall asleep at the wheel and crash their trucks. This is a reward-level accident.

UNIT 7   Part B

Exercise 1

I = interviewer
PV = Pío Verges

I   Mr Verges, what would you say are the rules of negotiation?

PV   Number one: you can't negotiate everything. I believe that negotiating is a specific task for a specific field. Being able to negotiate purchasing from hospital suppliers doesn't make you capable of negotiating the terms of a long-term loan with banks, for example. In fact, I believe most people are probably incapable of negotiating both effectively. What I mean to say by this is that there's a trend to make people believe that just because they know how to negotiate in one area they can negotiate anything. I think this is one of the concepts that has been overworked by the press, the publishers, with the intention of selling more books about negotiation. In my experience, it takes quite a long time for a person to develop negotiating skills in a certain field because he or she has to be or become a specialist in that field. Once a person knows how to negotiate within a specific field, he or she may feel totally awkward or incapable of negotiating in other fields.

I   Rapport is also important, isn't it?

PV   Generally you try to build up a positive feeling and a good atmosphere during the negotiations. But you have to know when to say "no" and when to be tough … and very often, what you're negotiating is pure greed on behalf of both parties and one party, the stronger one, is usually the one that tries to impose itself, because it wants to earn more money.

I   To what extent do you have to put yourself in the other person's shoes when you're negotiating?

PV   Well, it's very difficult to quantify that, but I would say, at least 50 per cent. You have to understand the other person's needs, their objectives. You also need to know the status they have in the organisation. How much authority do they have? How much autonomy do they really have? What experience do they have? and so on.

I How does negotiating change when you're dealing with somebody from a different country or culture?

PV I think that negotiation is smoother when both parties are of the same culture, and it's more efficient. I also think it's always necessary, in a transcultural situation, if you're from different cultures, to have somebody from the other culture as an advisor, somebody to lean on, to tell you what the pros and cons or the hidden messages of the negotiation with the other culture are.

Exercise 2

1 Yes, well, we've just analysed feedback on the course and the results are very satisfying. Eighty per cent of the participants said that they would repeat the course, 92 per cent said that they would recommend it. There was almost unanimous agreement regarding the usefulness of the course for those involved in foreign trade. However, many participants, nearly a third in fact, felt that a weekend was too short and a further 22 per cent said that they really needed more in-depth analysis rather than an overview and a third felt that in-company courses would be beneficial …

2 I don't think we'll ever think the same way about the way other people do things again. For years we just presumed our way was better and we couldn't understand those who didn't do things like we did. Seeing it all on film and on the computer made it so much more real. The lectures and discussion groups were great, but seeing it and working with interactive material made it sink in, somehow. I can see how our negotiating tactics are going to have to change …

3 Now as part of the sales drive this year we've decided that apart from technical preparation, many of you could benefit from brushing up your negotiating skills. I'm told the course is extremely practical and you'll be shown how to judge potential clients – and yourself – and guide the sales negotiation in the right direction. We really feel this is an investment and that you personally and the company as a whole will benefit from it. The course will be held here, one day to start with, and the dates and times are on your schedule. Now are there any questions?

UNIT 8 Part A

Exercise 1

The first thing to remember about market research is that it's really difficult, if not impossible, for one person, or even a group of people, to anticipate what is in the public's mind. Market research is used when you want to know what the public is thinking or how the public will behave, and you have the humility to know that you can't possibly, personally, know this without some research data.

Some specific examples of companies that have used market research come to mind. One example would be the coffee industry. There came a point in time when the industry noticed there was a decline in coffee consumption and nobody really knew why. They just were aware of the fact that fewer pounds of coffee were being purchased in the marketplace. They decided to carry out a survey of consumers, and a questionnaire was designed to find out how people were spending their day: what they were doing, what they were eating, and what they were drinking. And it didn't take long to discover that social habits were changing. People were no longer sitting around having a cup of coffee, but were more on the go and at the same time as consumption of coffee was declining, consumption of soft drinks was increasing, reflecting a change in lifestyles.

Market research is also used a lot by companies trying to reach the public through advertising. Broadcasting a 60-second or 30-second TV commercial can cost hundreds of thousands or even millions of dollars. What should the copy be? What should the people in the commercial be saying? What will be remembered? What points does the manufacturer want to make in the ad? Testing out several alternatives, exposing a sample of people to each of the different commercials and then asking them what they recall will quickly reveal which of the points being made are remembered and which are forgotten.

Another interesting case where market research was used was that of an automobile manufacturer, testing out a new car model with potential purchasers of the car. The reaction to the car was that it was sluggish and had no power. The manufacturer knew that this was not the case as the car engine was particularly strong and had a considerable amount of horsepower. We then undertook a qualitative study, a smaller, more in-

depth kind of look, with a small panel of consumers. Through this study, we discovered that the accelerator pedal was really stiff and it required a considerable amount of effort to push it down. This left the driver of the car with the feeling that it required a lot of effort to cause the car to go fast, to accelerate, which led to his or her impression that the car was sluggish.

Those are just a few examples. The underlying point and the reason, the basic reason for market research is that you can't sit in your chair and think that you know what a cross-section of the public thinks about your product, a television commercial, a candidate for political office, the taste of a product, or what a good colour for a package would be. One person can't represent the entire universe of people that are potential users of a product.

Exercise 2

I = interviewer
WN = Wayne Newton

I And on our programme this evening we're going to talk to someone who created a business, found his niche, watched in horror as it nearly disappeared overnight into the hands of booksdirect.com, but has managed to hold his own. Wayne, how did you start out?

WN Well, I've always been an outdoors person. Now, I found that it wasn't always easy to get books on places I wanted to go to, or about activities I wanted to do, so I set up a mail-order catalogue business specialising, and I mean *really* specialising, in books for adventurous travellers.

I Books for adventurous travellers? Are there enough people … I mean is the market big enough, and easy enough to reach to be able to make a living?

WN You'd be surprised just how big certain niche markets can be. Often the market isn't big enough to be able to open a retail outlet, but mail-order can work very well.

I But then you went on-line, didn't you? How did that come about?

WN Yeah, at first it was mail-order only, then we were invited to feature as an on-line link, you know, on somebody's web page, which we felt was worth the try, and orders trickled in. It was only a book or two a day at first, but that was a good start, and we did get an inkling as to what could be done on the internet. Then we were approached by a really avant-garde internet outfit, BASOL, and they were offering a much more comprehensive service in return for a commission. The commission seemed reasonable enough, so we accepted the deal and sales soared to 20 or 30 orders a day.

I That's a big jump, isn't it?

WN Yeah. We were doing really rather well; we'd found our niche, were exploiting it quite successfully, between the mail-order business and the internet; and then almost overnight it was grabbed, stolen if you like, by booksdirect.com.

I Oh goodness!

WN Yes, quite – it was all rather disconcerting to say the least. What we suspected was happening was that people were consulting our catalogue, available through this internet company, and then buying at booksdirect for 20 per cent less. Now the company we were working with was getting about 900,000 hits a month at the time, and we realised that to keep our market, or rather to get it back, we were going to have to add something to the product we were offering. In other words we were going to have to sell solutions, not products or services. We were also going to have to educate our customers so that they could get the most out of what we were offering and act almost like a partner, creating an enjoyable customer experience and an appreciation of the fact that price is not everything.

I That sounds ambitious. What exactly did you do?

WN Well, we started offering books that booksdirect didn't, like rare editions, books from tiny or even obscure publishers, and so on. In other words, we differentiated our product range. Another example of this diversification is products like signed posters that booksdirect aren't interested in. We also set up an intricate network of links to sites related to the outdoors and travel. We have a fortnightly newsletter and customers can talk to or e-mail our staff about their own journeys and adventures.

I Is that why you employ people who climb mountains, cross deserts, trek in the jungle; people who go sailing, white-water rafting, bungee-jumping, hang-gliding, and so on?

WN That's right, they add their expertise to our service. A person without that kind of experience can't relate to our customers' needs or answer their questions.

I   I believe you now have a shop as well as a website, haven't you?

WN   That's right – that bookshop we could never have set up at the outset is now there, and customers come from afar to meet us. It's part of our way of marketing within the niche, public relations. People are willing to pay for it, too, which is why we've bounced back.

I   Well, I'm sure many of our listeners will be wanting to ask you questions and indeed we've already received a stack of e-mails, so after the break, it's question time …

UNIT 9   Part B

Exercises 1 and 2

1 April 16th. Veronica Smythe calls Simon Gale.

SG   Sales Department, Simon Gale speaking.

VS   Good afternoon, Mr Gale. This is Veronica Smythe from Lassaters here. We've just received your e-mail confirming our order for the computers, but there seems to be a mistake. We wanted 500 computers, not 900.

SG   Oh dear, I am sorry. Let me have a look. Ah. Right, I've corrected that now. I'll make all the adjustments and you'll get confirmation in an hour or so.

VS   Thank you very much.

SG   Thank you for pointing out the mistake. We'll be in touch just before delivery.

VS   Fine. Goodbye, Mr Gale.

SG   Goodbye.

2 April 19th. Peter MacFarnan calls Toni Fiorello.

TF   Peter, what's up? I'm in a meeting.

PM   Well, Toni, the factory's e-mailed us to say production's been held up on the N745s.

TF   Why?

PM   Well, some parts haven't arrived. The logistics firm said heavy rains are to blame … and the weather's not likely to change for at least a couple of days.

TF   Oh dear. They should've informed us about the delay. How many orders do we have for the N745s on our books?

PM   Well we have the 500 for Lassaters and –

TF   Oh no, not Lassaters! That's a big order and an important one. Perhaps we can re-route the parts or use an alternative supplier.

PM   That might take time and it won't be cheap. Should we call Lassaters to let them know?

TF   No, we should let Susan Cleaver know first. She's in charge of these things. And we'd better check our agreement with Transglo, the logistics people – we may be insured against this. Can you check that out?

PM   Sure, talk to you later.

3 April 22nd. Veronica Smythe calls Nelson Computers.

NC   Sales Department, can I help you?

VS   Can I speak to Simon Gale, please?

NC   I'm afraid he's not in the office. Would you like to leave a message?

VS   Well, maybe you can help. This is Veronica Smythe from Lassaters Hotels here. We ordered 500 N745s just over a week ago on the understanding that they would be delivered within a week. Can you tell me when we can expect this delivery, please?

NC   I'm sorry, I don't have that information. I'll leave a message for Mr Gale to call you when he gets back, if you like.

VS   Well, isn't there anyone else who can give me this information?

NC   Er … Well … I don't know.

VS   Can you reach Mr Gale on his mobile phone? This is very urgent.

NC   I'm not sure.

VS   Please try, this is urgent.

NC   I'll see what I can do.

4 April 24th. Veronica Smythe calls Nelson Computers.

NC   Nelson Computers, can I help you?

VS   Yes, this is Veronica Smythe of Lassaters here. Listen, we ordered 500 of your N745s and we were promised we would have the computers here within a week – and that's ten days ago.

NC   One moment, I'll put you through to Sales.

VS   No, no, no. I spoke to Sales two days ago to ask about the situation and nobody there seemed to know what was going on. I sent a letter as well and haven't received a reply. I need to speak to someone else.

NC   Well, just one moment, I'll put you through to Peter MacFarnan in Logistics then.

VS   Thank you.

NC   *[pause]* I'm afraid the line's busy. Will you hold?

VS   No, can you ask him to call me, please? This is urgent.

5 April 24th. Peter MacFarnan calls Veronica Smythe at Lassaters.

L   Lassaters, Purchasing Department, good morning.

PM   Good morning, this is Peter MacFarnan from Nelson Computers here. Can I speak to Veronica Smythe, please?

L   I'm afraid she's in a meeting at the moment. Can I take a message?

PM   Yes, it's about your order for 500 N745s.

L   Yes, I know the situation. Any news?

PM   Good news, fortunately. We'll be able to deliver the computers the day after tomorrow, first thing in the morning.

L   Oh, I am glad. Oh, here's Veronica now. I think it's better if you sort things out with her.

UNIT 10   Part B

Exercise 1

Good morning. On behalf of the organising committee I'd like to welcome you all to our two-day knowledge management seminar.

Many years ago, in the late seventies, a university professor of mine, Dr Robert Dickler, said, "In the future, power will depend very much on information. Access to information will distinguish the haves from the have-nots."

That is still very much the case; indeed, bringing information through the internet to the developing nations is a major ongoing challenge. Without a doubt, there is a "before" and "after" the widespread use of the internet by companies, organisations and individuals. We have always needed and used information; we have always needed and used knowledge; but the information society has revolutionised what we do and can do with information. At the touch of a button, we can now access an unlimited amount of data, much more than even most science fiction writers ever imagined.

When we were planning the programme for this seminar, we often talked about the extent to which our working lives had changed since the development of information technologies. The way this information can be converted into knowledge, into expertise, into an asset is one of the real challenges facing businesses and organisations today.

Without a doubt, the information society is having a profound effect on the way businesses are run. We have all had to or will have to change our mind-sets. That is why we are here today.

We've invited a range of keynote speakers and organisations to share their knowledge with us all. We hope you get a lot from the seminar. Before handing over now to Michael Albright, I would like to remind you of a Chinese proverb that says, "By filling one's head instead of one's pocket, one cannot be robbed."

Exercise 2

Part 1

Thank you, Sandra. Before handing the microphone over to Dr David Gordon, I'd like to point out a couple of changes to our programme and remind you of a few details. All changes have been posted on our website and on bulletin boards on each floor.

Unless otherwise announced, when there are two sessions at the same time, the first-mentioned talk in each time-slot will be held in the Charman Room, the second talk mentioned will be held in the Mansfield Room. When there is only one talk programmed it will be held in the Charman Room.

I'd like to remind you that all plenary sessions, panel and round-table discussions will be held here in the auditorium, as will any video or on-line conferences.

First of all a few general points. To give people time to change rooms, all sessions will start ten minutes after the time indicated on the programme. Latecomers will be unable to enter. If you do miss a session, remember that you can use your personalised password to access the event through our website.

Part 2

There have been a few additions and changes to the programme, which I would now like to mention.

First of all, unfortunately, because of the illness of the speaker, this afternoon's programmed session on keeping staff up-to-date has been cancelled.

Today's 3 pm session entitled "Making the Most out of Know-how" will now be held in the auditorium and not in the Charman Room. The round-table discussion following it at 4.30 will no longer be on the principles underlying KM but will be on staff training.

Tomorrow morning at 8.30 there will be an additional talk entitled "Nurturing Employees", which examines the relationship between low staff turnover, productivity and profit. This will be held in the Mansfield Room.

Software, knowledge management and staff training consultants have set up displays so that you can see for yourselves what is available. You will find the latter two in the main foyer and the former in the annexe and on the first floor.

Remember that on each floor there is an information booth, as well as a café and lounge area where you can relax and share ideas.

You can get mobile phones and laptops recharged if you need to at the information booth.

By the way, the dinner-dance this evening will be held in the Royal Tasman Hotel, in Blenheim Place in the heart of the city. Anyone still interested in attending can reserve at the information booths until 11.45 or on-line until 12.30.

And now, a few words about Dr David Gordon ...

UNIT 11 Part A

Exercise 1

> I = interviewer
> RG = Rata Grace

I   And in Morocco yesterday, former Prime Minister Mike Moore, as expected, made an unequivocal speech in which he reiterated his view that the liberalisation of trade has to continue and that it must bring real benefits to all countries, particularly to the least developed nations. To give us more details, here's Rata Grace. Good morning, Rata.

RG Good morning, Jo.

I   Any surprises after Mr Moore's speech?

RG Well, not really. After all, the organisation he represents does stand for progressive trade liberalisation, enforceable rules and negotiated commitments. The day Moore came to office he called upon the developed nations to open their markets, to bring the poorest nations into the multilateral trading system and to bring more technical co-operation. Moore is insistent that there be duty-free access for any product whatsoever coming from the least developed nations.

I   Did he talk much about the problems this attitude might give rise to?

RG Yes, Jo, he said that the world in many ways has moved from a feeling of apathy to a feeling of anxiety, sometimes even anger, as far as free trade is concerned. On the one hand, you have a series of countries, like India, that feel that they have been locked out for far too long. On the other hand, there are countries, particularly developed nations, that fear for their security, that are afraid of what opening the doors to cheaper products might do to their own home industries.

I   Rata, what about the growing gap between the rich countries and the poor ones? Did he mention that?

RG Well, he did and he didn't; he stated that the economic situation of many developing countries had not improved as much as had been expected, and that our thinking had changed.

I   In what way has our thinking changed?

RG Many people now realise that the liberalisation of financial and trade relations has to be managed in a way that also guarantees stability. You see, the LDCs, the least developed countries, are largely dependent on a small number of export products. When there's a crisis like the oil crisis in the seventies or the Asian Crisis, prices for raw materials fall and then internal demand falls. Indeed, this occurred in many of these least developed countries and led to political instability, growing poverty and so on. Moore regards political stability as being fundamental; without it, he says, there'll be no investment.

I   So what's the solution?

RG There needs to be better income distribution, within countries as well as among countries. Trade, according to Moore, will not answer all the problems, but it will help, so long as all countries receive real benefit and that this benefit is shared not squandered. He also said that technical assistance was a must and that there could never be enough of it.

I   Did he deal with any sectors in particular?

RG Well, as always, textiles and agriculture were on the agenda. Tariffs are still too high, and one of the other problems is that these sectors, particularly agriculture, are not doing too well, even in the developed nations, so there may well be resistance to changing the rules.

I   And sometimes the rules don't seem to be the same for everyone.

RG Indeed. Moore said that he wanted rules to become more useful and practical for developing countries. At present, rules are not always workable and Moore pointed out that arbitration was more costly to some countries than to others, which was unfair and had to be corrected.

I   Can you sum up the key ideas in a few words for us, Rata?

RG Well, first of all, trade is a means to an end, not an end in itself. Secondly, trade will raise standards of living if things are done fairly. In other words, market access will not be able to do the job on its own; the backing of capital, training, infrastructure and solid, sound governments are essential to real progress.

I   Meaningful words indeed. Thank you, Rata.

Exercise 2

> I = interviewer
> AB = Armand Basi

I   In the textile sector there is often a lot of talk about free trade and protectionism. How have things changed?

AB Well, in the world of textiles, protectionism is still to be found, mainly in those countries in which the textile industry is part of the basic economic structure. The world is heading, though, to complete liberalisation of the markets. In Spain, for example, the textile sector has always been very important and yet the market has been a free one for a number of years.

I   Does the world market, the globalised marketplace, offer guarantees to the consumer? Is it good for everyone?

AB Well, globalisation is, in fact, a result of modern means of communication. So, it is, really, a trend that simply cannot be stopped in a world of freedom and democracy. And depending on the type of product and the local circumstances, countries will be affected in one way or another.

I   But are consumer rights guaranteed?

AB That's a big question. I think that in the long term, the consumer will be the king, as we say here. There may be moments when there's a loss of quality, but in the end the balance between, the search for the best relationship between quality and price will be decisive. If a manufacturer or distributor accepts inferior quality, they run the risk of loss of image, and that can be very costly indeed.

I   What do you see as being the future of the textile industry in the more industrialised countries?

AB Well, to be honest, I think that some of the predictions made a few years back will not come about. You see, many people thought the global division of labour would lower costs and that factories would move depending on the competitive advantage one country or another had to offer. But in fact the reality can be costly and complex. The key, nowadays, is to get your product to market as fast as possible. The logistics involved in globalising the manufacturing processes are complex: shipping, timing, co-ordination and distribution. I mean, you can't airfreight, it's too costly. In addition, when you set up plants in other countries, you need to have your own technical staff on site, which involves additional costs – accommodation expenses – no, it's not working out the way some people had anticipated and I don't think it ever will.

I   So what do you think will happen?

AB I think, quite sincerely, that the future of the textile industry in the more developed nations lies precisely in the area of industrialisation – innovation, the creation of new materials and fabrics, new machines, creative design, the manufacturing of items with high added value, and agile service. In other words, reaching the consumer quickly means keeping the consumer satisfied. Only the industrialised nations can, at present, have the resources available to innovate in this way. The contribution of the developing nations will be limited to labour.

UNIT 12 Part B

Exercises 1, 2 and 3

I = interviewer
RC = revenue commissioner

Part 1

I How do you decide who to audit, who is going to be inspected?

RC The most efficient way is to do a pre-selection. We have a lot of outside information and through information systems, through the use of computers, we are able to determine what we call tax risk situations.

I For example?

RC For example, let's say we have a list of people that bought a very expensive car, like a Ferrari, last year. At the same time we have their tax returns. We are able to say: if what they are saying is the truth, only x number of people have been able to buy a car like this and this person is or is not one of them. Our information systems detect such anomalies. So, that would be a very simple way to decide whom we inspect.

I How exactly do you detect these anomalies – through outside information?

RC Yes, we receive information through banks and through other financial institutions; we may know, for example, if you have invested, if you have sold something and what you have earned via this transaction. These operations may or may not be reflected in your tax returns. A very simple spot audit detects this. We may undertake really thorough investigations. These are not so simple. We may have been tipped off – something may have happened – and this is not so straightforward. It may mean that we go through your numbers, we go through your books, we go through additional information, we do studies of different contracts and that is really what we call investigation.

I And are such investigations more likely to be with companies or with individuals?

RC Companies, certainly. Although there are several people, several individuals with a high income, or high net-worth individuals, who may be considered very high risk. And there are people who simply do things that are considered high risk, and then they are also put under thorough investigation.

I You mentioned cars, and information received from third parties; what other indicators are there?

RC People whose income varies a lot, or is not given to us by third parties such as employers and banks. These are people whose data we can't work on in the pre-selection stage.

I You mean the self-employed?

RC Or companies that do sophisticated operations like mergers or buyouts.

I And what percentage of the population is investigated at some time in their lives?

RC It's difficult to say, because there are different degrees of investigation. If we look at all the variations, I would say it may be around 40 per cent of the population at some stage or another. Thorough investigation is much less than that.

Part 2

I You've talked about who is inspected and why. Tell me, how have things changed over the years?

RC Well, tax evasion is getting more and more sophisticated.

I Why is that?

RC Well, we now have much more control than we used to. Ten or fifteen years ago we didn't have as much information. We didn't have the methods or instruments to gather and control information. Now, we've got a lot of information and can control it better through IT. Therefore, the way people evade taxes has become, has had to become more sophisticated, it's not so straightforward anymore.

I You mean double bookkeeping, tax havens…

RC Off-shore companies, fictitious companies that open and close overnight and many more methods, I assure you. Controlling that is not simple. You see, we have a global economy, yet inland revenues are divided into countries, or even within a country. When you've got a frontier, your work gets more complicated. For example, to control any activity done abroad, we need international co-operation. Although international co-operation has increased a lot in the last five years, it's still not the usual way to work.

I And will this change, do you think?

RC When you consider how many companies are working in different countries and how easily they do so, ah, I think that what we will need to do in the next few years, will be precisely to get better at co-ordinating the different inland revenue services in different countries. The OECD recently decided to take a hard line with some tax havens, but bank secrecy is still there. We are also going to face the challenge of how to tax in cyberspace. That is a whole new area.

Exercises 4 and 5

1 What usually happens is that we have two different budgets. On the one hand we're given sales targets. We're told that we're expected to sell x amount of computers or y amount of modems by a certain date. At the same time we're allotted an expense account to achieve those objectives. Every quarter we have to file a performance report in which we assess whether these objectives are being achieved. So if our sales figures are lower than those forecast, we have to justify why this is so and if we're spending too much, likewise. The end of the quarter is often a stressful time, especially when the targets were too optimistic.

2 We've changed the way we budget. Instead of being given objectives and being told how much we could spend and how many new accounts we should aim to open, we now do what's called "grassroots budgeting". So each branch decides, "This is what we think we can realistically achieve and these are the additional resources we will need to achieve these objectives." In the branch itself we all sit around and talk about how we can use our present resources better and how we might be able to grow. We might decide that if we had another automatic teller, for example, we'd be able to sell more pension schemes and so on. The branch manager then discusses the forecasts with head office and an agreement is reached. We're all involved now and feel quite positive about the change.

3 I don't know how the company budgets overall. I'm only involved in projects. But with bridges and buildings, we usually have to submit an estimate or a tender, if bids have been called for, in which we state quite categorically what we intend to build, how long it will take and how much it will cost. So when we make our calculations, we have to predict and allow for increases in the cost of materials, labour and so on. Once we start working we have to keep a tight control of costs so as not to go over the budgeted amount, which right now is really difficult because there's a boom in the industry and qualified labour is scarce and consequently expensive. Bricklayers are earning as much as I am.

4 We have six manufacturing divisions and each is responsible for its own profit planning and control – that's a fancy name for budgeting. We have monthly meetings in which the product division controllers compare how things are going and give advice to each other about handling problems. It's really good because you can learn a lot from others. Mind you, each division is a world of its own and even though they're all made of steel, products differ greatly. The head of control and finance sits in on the meetings and pinpoints aspects to work on or points out major deviations from what we call the "master plan", which is the company budget as a whole. Last month it was inventory. We all had a little more stock than the planned level. In total, though, the value was significant.

5 Basically, we're given a budget, an allocation really, and we're told: "Squeeze as much as you can out of it." Hospital technology is moving fast and equipment is expensive, but instead of paying outright or leasing, new machines are paid for in instalments, so the end cost of each machine is far higher than it would have been. We're still paying for machines bought four years ago, now semi-obsolete. We can't afford to buy technology we ought to have, let alone do medical research. That makes it hard to do a good job and give proper service. Sometimes we manage to reduce expenditure, but often, cheaper materials are not really cheaper at all. A couple of years ago, they decided to buy cheaper catheters. The quality was so poor, they kept on breaking, and we had to replace them. We ended up spending 50 per cent more on catheters.

Answer key

A Reading

2
1 b 2 b 3 c 4 d 5 a 6 b

B Listening and reading

1
1 T 2 T 3 F 4 T 5 T 6 F

2
1 200
2 managers
3 senior managers
4 20
5 super grads/super graduates
6 general manager(s)
7 graduates
8 (academic) results/grades/marks
9 not important/of no consequence
10 social activities/sports activities/social events

4
1 A, B 2 A 3 C 4 A, B 5 C
6 A 7 A, B

5
1 A 2 C 3 B

6
a 3 b 2 c ✗ d ✗ e 1

UNIT 2

KEY VOCABULARY
1 lending agency
2 cash flow
3 Cash flow management
4 breaking even
5 Premises

A Reading

2
A BUSINESS START-UPS: THE FACTS
B THE CAUSES OF FAILURE
C HOW TO START
D PLANNING IS ESSENTIAL
E THE CONTENTS OF A BUSINESS PLAN
F SOURCES OF ADVICE

4
The best summary is b.

B Listening

KEY VOCABULARY
1 B 2 F 3 A 4 E 5 D 6 C
7 H 8 G

1
1 A 2 B 3 G 4 F 5 C

2
a 4 b 1 c 3 d 1 e 2 f 5
g 3 h 4 i 2 j 5

3
A ✗ B 1 C 5 D 2 E 3 F 4

C Speaking and writing

1 *Model questions*
1 When was the company founded?/When did the company start up?
2 What type of company was it initially?
3 How long has it been a public company?
4 Has the company grown steadily or have there been ups and downs?/How would you describe the way the company has grown?
5 Did going public lead to significant changes in terms of growth?
6 Where are the bicycles manufactured?/Where are the factories located?
7 What is the company's distribution network like?
8 What are their aims/plans for the immediate future?
9 Are they planning to launch any new products in the (near) future?/Will they be launching any new models in the (near) future?/Do they have any new products on the drawing board?

2 *Model questions*
1 Do you know when the company was founded?/Can you tell me when the company started up?
2 Do you know what type of company it was initially?
3 Do you know how long it has been a public company?
4 Do you know if the company has grown steadily, or have there been ups and downs?
5 Can you tell me whether going public led to significant changes in terms of growth?
6 Can you tell me where the bicycles are manufactured/where the factories are located?
7 Can you tell us something about their distribution network?
8 Do you know what their aims/plans for the immediate future are?
9 Do you know if they are planning to launch any new products in the (near) future?/Do you know if they will be launching any new models in the (near) future?/Can you tell me if they have any new products on the drawing board?

4
a, c, f, e, d, b

5 *Model press release*
Zara, flagship of the Inditex group of companies, is a growing chain of retail fashion outlets. Stores operate world-wide and receive new merchandise twice a week, delivered by a large fleet of trucks and aircraft.

Inditex started up in 1963 in Galicia, Spain. Its major shareholder and founder is Amancio Ortega. Zara opened its first shop in 1975 and has grown steadily since then. By 1998, the group owned 740 outlets. Between 1985 and 1999 turnover went from 30 million euros to 2 billion euros. They employed 12,000 people in 1997, 9% more than in the previous year. Sustained growth, a more developed retail network across Europe and further expansion world-wide are planned for the future.

UNIT 3

A Reading and writing

KEY VOCABULARY
a) turnkey operations
b) targeted at
c) add-ons
d) outsourcing
e) sales pitch

1
1 c 2 b 3 a 4 b 5 c 6 c
7 a 8 c 9 b 10 d 11 d
12 c 13 c 14 d

2 *Model executive summary*
REPORT ON THE SECOND ANNUAL MEDICAL CONVENTION

Executive Summary

The purpose of this report, requested by the Board of Directors, is to analyse feedback on the convention and to compare it with last year's event.

FINDINGS
Levels of satisfaction with the convention have risen on the whole. Changing the criteria for selecting speakers, accommodation and catering should improve the standard of the convention in the future.

1. *Venue and activities*
Participants appreciated this year's change of venue to a better-equipped centre and the more participant-oriented programme of activities offered (80% satisfaction compared with 30% last year).

2. *Stands and displays*
Stands and displays were more visible this year. Consequently, more feedback was provided (95% response compared with 75% last year). Most of the increased response was favourable, ie levels of dissatisfaction remain fairly stable (25%, 20%).

3. *Speakers and content*
People were less impressed by the invited speakers and what they had to say this year. Whereas last year nearly 40% felt that the standard of speakers was high, this year only 5% held this opinion.

4. *Food and accommodation*
The number of participants who rated these poor doubled this year, from around 10% to around 20%. Requests have been made for greater variety in the menus (including vegetarian food) and for better facilities in the hotel (eg gymnasium).

CONCLUSIONS AND RECOMMENDATIONS
Medical conventions continue to play an important public relations role in the COL

Pharmaceutical Group's marketing strategy. Feedback on this year's convention has in general been positive. The following improvements are recommended:
• invite more well-known speakers
• use a hotel with sports facilities
• negotiate menus to cater for vegetarians, etc

B Reading and listening
1
1 B   2 D   3 C   4 A   5 A
2
1 C – after   3 D – before
2 B – at   4 A – at
3
1 b   2 b   3 a   4 a   5 c   6 a

C Speaking
3
The best alternative(s) are the following:
1 a, b   2 b   3 a   4 a   5 a, c   6 a

UNIT 4

KEY VOCABULARY
1 b   2 f   3 e   4 a   5 c   6 d

A Listening and writing
1
1 F   2 H   3 C   4 A   5 E
2
a 2   b 5   c ✗   d 4   e 1   f 3
g ✗   h ✗

4 *Model answer*
To: ducatissimo@euol.com
From: WebstersFashion@ukol.com
Subject: Special limited offer

Dear Paola,
Thank you for your e-mail of -/-/-. The answer is yes, we would like to look at this range. As you know, our experience with these offers has been positive to date.

We would be able to meet Mr Guido at our offices on Thursday morning at 8.30 or on Friday at 11 am. Please let us know how long it will take to see the collection and discuss matters so that we can shift appointments if necessary. As we have a particularly tight schedule this week we would be grateful if Mr Guido could arrive on time.

There are a few details we need to sort out before making a purchasing decision:
1 Labels. Can you guarantee that the labels will be in English?
2 Delivery. Can you guarantee delivery by Easter? If the goods do not arrive until mid-May we will need to negotiate special conditions such as the right to cancel the order.
3 Sizes and quantities. Can you please give us a preview of sizes and models available? Are there any complete ranges available, or only odd sizes?

We also need more information on minimum quantities, discounts on larger orders, and so on.

Please get back to us on the above by Wednesday to confirm the appointment.

With best wishes,

Josephine

B Reading
1
1 c   2 a   3 a   4 b   5 d   6 b
7 d   8 c   9 a   10 c
3
1 D   2 A   3 B   4 C   5 C   6 A
5
A – both
B – both (though targeted more at individuals)
C – individuals
D – businesses

C Speaking
2
1 D   2 B   3 A   4 E   5 C
4
1 Her speech is about two minutes long.
2 She starts by saying what her speech will be about.
3 Yes, she does.
4 No, she doesn't.
5 She mentions the following points: a, c, b, e

UNIT 5

KEY VOCABULARY
2 short-term loan
3 long-term loan
4 stock market
5 bear market/bull market
6 current account
7 pension plan

A Listening
1
1 ✗   2 ✓   3 ✗   4 ✗   5 ✓
2
a 4   b 2   c 1   d 3   e 5   f 5
4
1 b   2 a   3 a   4 a   5 c   6 c
7 b   8 b

B Reading
1
1 b   2 a   3 c   4 c   5 a   6 d
7 a   8 b   9 c   10 b   11 c   12 d
13 a   14 c   15 d
3
1 risen – raised
2 supplies – suppliers
3 These – This
4 so – to
5 independents – independence
6 investments – investors
7 Much – Many/Most
8 entirely – entire
9 done – made
10 a – an

C Speaking and writing
2 *Model answer*
Dear _____,
We *[who? – state who you are and what you do/what you are planning to do]*. We know that you invest in projects with imagination, drive and a promising future. Your reputation for spotting and supporting potentially successful ventures is second to none. *[state name, eg Our accountants]* believe that you will be interested in our

venture and have recommended that we approach you to obtain seed capital.

We are enclosing a detailed business plan and hope you will include our project within your investment portfolio. We believe that the investment is a sound one. Our business mission is clear. The operating budgets and cash-flow forecasts are realistic and all market research undertaken has been favourable.

Our project has been approved by the authorities and will be receiving some financial assistance in the first three months. To ensure a successful start-up, *[what? – repeat the name of the company]* requires an additional injection of *[how much as a percentage of total capital?]* capital. According to our calculations, the venture should break even *[when?]* and there are considerable possibilities for expanding the business.

As a team we have a combination of appropriate experience and entrepreneurial qualities, details of which are outlined in the enclosed plan.

We would very much like to discuss our proposal with you in person within the next month. We can be contacted at *[say where and when you can be contacted; give phone/fax number, e-mail address, etc]*.

Yours sincerely,

UNIT 6

A Listening
1
1 a   2 c   3 b   4 c   5 c   6 b
2
1 operators
2 Systems
3 construction sites
4 safety platforms
5 Job rotation
6 (safety) experiments were
7 scientists from Moscow/senior civil servants
8 lack of/poor
9 8–10 per cent
10 speak different languages
11 ten or twelve
12 truck drivers

B Reading
1
1 D   2 A   3 E   4 C   5 B
6 D   7 C   8 E
2
1 owing/due/related
2 which/that
3 how
4 between
5 When
6 rather
7 through/by
8 Not
9 results
10 greater/higher/increased/better

C Speaking and writing
1
Model answers
1b The staff were asked whether they received regular retraining and they

commented that they had received none since the safety officer had left.

1c We asked the staff if the crisis management procedures were familiar to all. They said that they were, but that these procedures had not been revised for five years.

2a Our first impression, when we examined the kitchens to see whether they were clean, was positive. However, upon closer examination we found bacteria and dirt in the corners.

2b We checked the ventilation of the kitchens and observed that the extractors had been poorly maintained.

2c When we checked the temperature, the results were uneven: it was too hot in some areas and too cold in others.

3a Cutting machine were inspected one by one: not all machines had a guard. When we asked why, we were told that guards had been removed because they had become loose.

3b When we inspected staff clothing, we noticed that on the whole, clothing was very worn, showing signs of wear and tear such as holes and stains.

3c We examined whether hazardous areas were clearly recognisable or not and they were correctly signed.

4a We checked whether all cooking utensils had been properly cleaned or not and they had been.

4b The state of the floors, walls and ceilings was checked: paint was peeling in a number of areas and there were several cracks.

4c Examination of the cleanliness of the floors, walls, benches and other fittings uncovered several signs of the presence of beetles and mice on the premises and considerable residual bacteria in the cracks.

5a We found that the workstations were poorly designed. Some of the fixtures on cupboards and racks were unsafe.

5b Forearms were rarely parallel to the ground. The tables were too low and most staff were having to bend excessively.

UNIT 7

A Reading

1
1 a 2 g 3 h 4 e 5 d 6 c
7 f

2
1 d 2 c 3 a 4 a

3
1 understanding
2 specifications
3 interrelationship/interrelation
4 judg(e)ment
5 shopper
6 awareness
7 concessions

B Listening and writing

1
1 c 2 a 3 b 4 c 5 b 6 b

2
1 A 2 D 3 B

3
Model answer
Dear _____ ,
Waytogo is a growing travel operator specialising in adventure holidays. We

currently operate in three continents and are about to expand into Africa. We are writing to request information about your Assertive Negotiation course.

Before making the decision to send employees on this course, we would like to have more details of the course content and conditions. Could you please e-mail us information specifying:
• the areas covered in the one-day seminar and the content of follow-up sessions
• the qualifications and experience of the speakers and teaching staff
• the dates and prices of the one-day seminars and follow-up sessions
• the minimum and maximum number of participants per seminar

We would also be interested in seeing references from people that have already been on the course.

Could you please send the information by December 6th.
Thank you in advance.

Best regards,

C Speaking

KEY EXPRESSIONS
1 i 2 h 3 b 4 d 5 f 6 a
7 c 8 e 9 g

UNIT 8

KEY VOCABULARY

1
The combinations most frequently used in marketing are:

brand study	niche market
brand loyal	product launch
brand researcher	product sales
market niche	sales commission
market researcher	sales study
market share	target market
market study	target niche

2
1 brand loyal
2 target market
3 niche market
4 market researcher/market study
5 product launch
6 market share
7 sales commission

A Listening

1
1 were falling/declining
2 soft drinks
3 changing lifestyles/changing social habits
4 a questionnaire
5 on television/on TV
6 which points/which messages
7 potential purchasers/potential buyers
8 was negative/was not good
9 less powerful
10 a stiff pedal/the accelerator pedal

2
1 b 2 c 3 a 4 b 5 b 6 c
7 a 8 c

B Speaking

KEY VOCABULARY
Column 1: drop
Column 2: hold steady
Column 3: bounce back (indicates significant change), peak (is upward movement heading towards a maximum point after which there is a change – normally noticeable), slide

1
Model answers
1 rose/went up/increased/climbed (steadily)
2 peaked/reached a peak
3 fell/went down (slightly)
4 plunged/plummeted/fell/went down/decreased (dramatically/significantly)
5 remained stable/remained constant/stabilised/levelled off/evened out

C Reading and writing

1
1 a 2 c 3 a 4 d 5 b 6 b
7 d 8 a 9 c 10 a 11 c 12 d

2
1 too 2 ✓ 3 ✓ 4 have 5 so
6 ✓ 7 With 8 the 9 ✓ 10 ✓
11 high 12 not 13 ✓ 14 which
15 ✓ 16 be 17 ✓ 18 them

UNIT 9

KEY VOCABULARY
1 h, i 2 f 3 c, e 4 b 5 g 6 d
7 a

A Reading

1
1 c 2 e 3 f 4 g 5 b

2
1 c 2 a 3 a 4 c 5 b

B Listening and writing

1
1 b 2 c 3 d 4 a 5 f

3
1 have
2 unable
3 have
4 they
5 up
6 improve/change
7 order
8 may/will
9 inform/advise
10 such

4 *Model letter of complaint*

Dear Ms Cleaver,
On April 14 we placed an order for 500 Nelson N745s confident that we would receive the goods within a week. Unfortunately we have yet to receive the computers and we have been unable to find out why.

This morning I called your sales department about the matter, but nobody seemed to know why the order had been delayed. In fact they were neither helpful nor understanding. We had planned to be able to set up our new computer system and have it running smoothly in time for the high season. The delay in the delivery of these computers is setting us back and placing us in a difficult situation as staff need training before the tourist season.

We trust you will appreciate that this delay is a matter of great concern to us and that a solution needs to be found promptly. Could you please let me know when the computers will arrive so that we can reschedule our training accordingly.

Yours sincerely,
Veronica Smythe
Purchasing Manager

Model reply

Dear Ms Smythe,
Thank you for your letter in which you expressed your concern at the delay in the delivery of your computers. We at Nelson Computers pride ourselves in being able to service orders within a week and indeed this is normally the case.

On this occasion, however, we have been unable to fulfil our promise as adverse weather conditions have held up components at their source. We apologise for this, but as you will appreciate, such events are beyond our control. You will be pleased to hear that we have managed to re-route these components and will have the computers ready within 48 hours.

We would also like to thank you for drawing our attention to the response of our sales department when you called to find out about the delay. You needed information. You were right to complain about receiving none.

Delays of this nature are most unusual in our company. We are using a new logistics company and our sales staff had not been informed about the situation. We have now reorganised our information-flow system so that this will not occur again.

We appreciate the inconvenience this delay has caused and would like to offer you our support when you are training your staff, should this be necessary. Our logistics department will be calling you later in the day to arrange delivery of the computers. Please let us know if there is anything else we can do for you.

Regards,
Susan Cleaver
Customer Services Director

C Speaking

KEY LANGUAGE
1 e   2 d   3 a   4 b   5 b   6 c
7 f   8 b   9 d   10 e

UNIT 10

A Reading

1
1 D   2 E   3 B   4 C   5 D   6 A
7 E   8 A

2
1 B   2 D   3 E   4 ✗   5 A   6 C

B Listening

1
1 T   2 T   3 F   4 T   5 F   6 T
7 T

2
Part 1
1 on the website
2 The sessions/talks
3 in the auditorium
4 ten minutes after
5 will be unable
6 can/must use

Part 2
1 cancelled
2 auditorium
3 staff training
4 Nurturing Employees
5 (in the) annexe, (on the) first floor
6 (in the) main foyer
7 on each floor
8 information booths
9 Royal Tasman Hotel (in Blenheim Place in the heart of the city)
10 (at) information booths until 11.45, on-line until 12.30

C Speaking and writing

KEY EXPRESSIONS
1 E   2 C   3 A   4 D   5 B

1
a 4   b 2   c 5   d 3   e 1

UNIT 11

KEY VOCABULARY
1 balance of payments
2 arbitrator
3 sanctions
4 surplus
5 dumping
6 quotas/protectionism

A Listening

1
1 T   2 F   3 T   4 F   5 T   6 T
7 T   8 T   9 T

2
1 b   2 c   3 a   4 c   5 c   6 b

B Reading

1
1 c   2 a   3 b   4 d   5 b   6 a
7 d   8 c   9 a   10 b

3 *First letter*
1 the   2 ✓   3 over   4 be   5 more
6 moreover   7 ✓   8 then   9 ✓
10 on

Second letter
1 has   2 though   3 being   4 ✓
5 for   6 the   7 ever   8 ✓   9 for
10 ✓

C Speaking and writing

KEY CONCEPTS
1 subsidies
2 Generous

3 include
4 payable/paid/payments
5 reduced
6 met
7 manufacturers
8 improving
9 industrial
10 employees

1
1 e   2 e   3 d   4 b   5 c   6 a
7 b   8 d   9 c   10 d

UNIT 12

KEY VOCABULARY
1 I   2 H   3 A   4 C   5 G   6 E
7 F   8 B   9 J   10 D

A Reading

1
1 advice   6 every
2 pride   7 wealth
3 minimise   8 havens
4 other   9 being
5 of   10 charged

2
1 b   2 a   3 b   4 d   5 c   6 b
7 a   8 d   9 b   10 a

B Listening

KEY VOCABULARY
1 + whose + F
2 + who/that + C
3 + that + E
4 + when + A
5 + which/that + H
6 + which/that + D
7 + when + G
8 + whose + B

1
1 T   2 T   3 F   4 T   5 T   6 F

2
1 b   2 a   3 a

KEY VOCABULARY
(if in brackets, possible, but less common)
1 make, file, submit, (keep)
2 submit, (file)
3 keep, achieve
4 achieve, reach
5 call
6 make, reach, achieve, submit
7 handle, make
8 reach, achieve, make, submit

4
1 F   2 B   3 C   4 G   5 E

5
a 5   b 1   c 3   d 2   e 4   f ✗

C Speaking and writing

KEY EXPRESSIONS
1 E (B, C)   2 C   3 A   4 D (B)   5 B
6 F (E)

DELTA Publishing
39 Alexandra Road
Addlestone
Surrey KT15 2PQ
United Kingdom

First published 2001
ISBN 1 900783 46 0,
        978-1-900783-46-0

Design and illustration by Oxford Designers & Illustrators
Printed in Malta by Progress Press Co. Ltd.

Author's acknowledgements
I would like to thank my editors Chris Hartley and Louise Elkins for showing me how to turn my ideas and manuscript into a usable course. Special thanks to my colleagues and students, particularly those at the European University, Barcelona, and at Empower Training, Barcelona, for piloting and commenting on the material.

I would also like to thank my business students (both present and past) for having provided me with so much information about their working worlds. For the listening material, I owe special thanks to: Svend Auken, Armand Basi, John Connolly, Tom Dwyer, Leonard Spector, Lilian Varela, Pío Vergés, and Xavier Vidal for providing me with original material to work with. Thanks also to Dr David Gordon, Claudio Loscertales, Reza Khoyi, Josep Artola, Esther Martin, Adolf Villacampa, Susan McGeary, Patrick McDonald and many others, who contributed with their business sense and experience.

Last but not least, thanks to my very patient family.

Photograph acknowledgements
The author and publishers wish to acknowledge, with thanks, the following photographic sources:

Art Directors and TRIP pp title (photograph S Grant); 5 (photograph S Grant); 30 (photograph C Rennie); 43 (photograph H Rogers); 45 (photograph J King); 62 (photograph J Greenberg); 74 (photograph Viesti Collection)

De Gracia p 65

PANOS Pictures pp 14 (photograph Chris Stowers); 54 (photograph Chris Stowers); 66 (photograph Philip Wolmuth)

Topham Picturepoint p 19 (photograph Martin Stephens)

Svend Auken (p 34)

The publishers have made every effort to trace the copyright holders, but if they have inadvertently overlooked any, they will be pleased to make the necessary arrangements at the first opportunity.